Reinvent YOU!

How to Move from "We" to "Me" after Divorce

Believe and Live Again

Zina Arinze

Reinvent You! How to Move from "We" to "Me" After Divorce. Believe and Live Again

Non-Fiction

Printed in the United Kingdom

First Printing 2017 Believe and Live Again Publishing

ISBN: 978-0-9955688-0-8

DEDICATION

My Father – God Almighty, my best friend, Confidant and Lover of my soul.

To every woman who has ever been lost, confused and in pain as a result of divorce, separation, relationship breakdown or domestic abuse, you deserve *to rewrite your own story, find joy and live the life you deserve*.

Jade and Crystal – My Gorgeous Princesses, gifts that keep giving me endless joy and happiness...if I had to do it all again, I would.
Love you both so madly, deeply.

My stoic, sacrificial, wise, fiercely protective and supportive Mummy – Ifeoma, I love you. If I could be even half of the woman that you are....

In loving memory of:

Lawrence Arinze – Unforgettable Daddy. Thank you for the "gift" you have instilled in me, I know you must be beaming with pride, I will always love you.

Dr Tayo Adeyemi – Pastor T *"Get something and put your name on it"* I did it!

Victoria Adeleye – Sis Toyin – Your love, support, prayers and 100% belief in me kept me going.

"What makes Zina's book so precious? She does not confine herself to providing you with practical information. If that was all you wanted and needed chances are, you would be able to get that from a government pamphlet.

"Reinvent You!" will tell you everything you need to know. But more than that, you will have Zina walking beside you along the journey, every step of the way. Zina, with all her vulnerability, wisdom and generosity, will be your guide."

– Dr Annie Kaszina,
Leading Women's Relationship Coach,
Speaker Award Winning Author

"This is an exceptional book. If I am pushed, I am prepared confess that this is a book that I wish that I'd written! Zina's style is humane, funny and real; this is a woman who has walked this journey and her passion to see others move on to thrive and believe and live again announces itself.

Not only is this an emotionally honest account of one woman's journey of self-discovery after the pain of divorce, it is a hugely inspiring book that escorts you from the bewilderment, uncertainty and self-doubt of relationship breakdown and allows you to position yourself in a place of confidence, hope and excitement about your future. Here, you will re-discover what you always knew but may have forgotten – that you are a capable, strong, resourceful and immensely valuable woman; not defined by her past but with a great and vibrant future ahead of her."

– Remi Gberbo,
Solicitor

"This book not only holds that vision, but does so with humor, honesty, and a deep sense of spirituality. It's the whole mind, body, spirit package that will serve you well through this life altering experience. Take time along the way to breathe and celebrate the small victories, such as not crying when your ex walks onto the field at your child's soccer game, or you standing up for yourself by setting a firm boundary.

Zina Arinze is the perfect guide to show you your way. May you be blessed with gifts of forgiveness and personal growth as your journey down this new path in your life."

– Lori S. Rubenstein, JD, PCC,
Author of "Forgiveness: Heal Your Past and Find the Peace You Deserve",
"Transcending Divorce", and "Freedom from Abuse"

ACKNOWLEDGEMENTS

"If you are lazy, and accept your lot, you may live in it.
If you are willing to work, you can write your name anywhere you choose."
– Gene Stratton-Porter, *A Girl of the Limberlost*

I would like to express my immense gratitude to all the wonderful, helpful, supportive people who have been involved in my book writing journey. For those of you who were my sounding boards, idea generators, stress relievers, tantrum controllers, researchers, proofreaders, voices of reason – I thank you. For the historians amongst you, filling in the blanks I had forgotten....I thank you. Forgive me if I have not mentioned you by name, know that in your own unique way you have been instrumental to ensuring that this book is now a reality. God bless you all.

In my first attempt at writing this, I had over 3000 words, a testament of how much I value and appreciate you individually and as a collective.

There are however a handful of people I would like to acknowledge specifically:

Olivia, what can I say, you were there before the beginning. Your love, friendship, sisterhood and encouragement remains a constant force. Thanks for being a much-needed sounding board for this book and keeping me sane – I love you so much.

Sophia Reid – my stoic energetic encourager, fiercely loyal, persistent – thank you *"the book is out."*

Morenike and Tessy – BFFs London Chapter, to the stars and beyond. ♥

I also wish to express my immense gratitude and thanks to my Book Journey Mentor – Daniella Blechner at Conscious Dreams Publishing for mentoring me through the book journey and publishing process. You saw, understood and believed in the vision to help as many women as possible successfully transition from the pain and grief associated with divorce, separation or the end of a relationship and with bulldog tenacity didn't let go or let me let go either. You have the patience of a saint; even when I had to literally rewrite the entire manuscript, you did not waver in your keen eye for details, legalities and support as well as in the management of my expectations, frustrations and my emotional meltdowns. You have been a God send. Apologies for the extra grey hairs. Thank you also for collaborating with the very able Lee Caleca as editors to edit, re-edit and go through the uncountable iterations both in editing and proofreading the manuscript again and again. Apologies for the added pressure by my always seeming to add that "one more chapter" after an edit.

I remain eternally grateful, thank you.

Nadia Vitushynska – my phenomenal typesetter who immediately caught my vision and used her incredible creative intuition and patience to give visual beauty and flow to each written word and phrase. Thank you.

To the truly amazing women from the Power of Your Story six-week Workshop, class of 2016. Afua, Corinna, Dionne, Donna, Khafi, Leah, Pauline, Prisca, Rebecca and Sandra – there is indeed safety in numbers, learning together and getting to know you and your stories is an incredible honour. (((Hugz)))

Embla Ester Granqvist – my wonderful and amazingly gifted illustrator, all I can say is Wow! You brought my book alive, thank you.

Pastor Michael, my New Wine Church Family and my home fellowship group in Woolwich, London – Thank you for the opportunity to serve, for your constant prayers, support, and encouragement and trust.

Dr Wole and Dami Olarinmoye – I will always cherish our friendship, your prayers and support on this project.

Bola Ogundeji -aka Mrs Echoes – Thank you for your friendship and of course the constant relentless reminder over the years *"Zina where is your book?"* Finally, I can heave a sigh of relief – DONE ✓

Eda Ziya – Thank you so much for those almost weekly gentle and not so gentle nudges as well as your supportive words of encouragement during the not so final lap. ☺

My 6am Sisters – Julie, Shade, Remi and Tracy, God knew. Thank you for being part of my journey and story.

Marcia Dixon – your support, friendship and encouragement has been phenomenal.

Sandra James – I will always cherish your encouragement, friendship and suggestions. Thank you for checking up on me from across the pond.

Dr Dee Adio Moses – you believed in me from the start, I will always cherish our cross country 1 to 1 coaching Skype calls, you stretched and guided me, and in 2011 encouraged me to write this book.....pay it forward 6 years later. ☺

Dr. Annie Kaszina – I will always cherish your integrity, humour, encouragement, friendship and generosity in sharing so freely your significant book writing experience.

Lori Rubenstein – My Learned colleague, Divorce Recovery Coaching Tutor and Friend – Thanking you for teaching me the ropes.

Julie Ziglar Norman – Your own life, integrity and wise counsel inspires me daily to be more and do more. Thank you.

Pastor Allen and my fellow presenters at Kent Christian Radio – Thank you.

Norva Samoy Abiona, AKA the Wise Wife – Author and friend, your daily check-in calls, advise, encouragement and book journey knowledge sharing has been invaluable.

My Believe and Live Again team – Job, Duska, Dooda, Palesa, Dorcas, Patrick, and Marva, you are indeed the best.

My awesome brothers, **Lawrence, Tim, Chuck** and my phenomenal little sister **Obi** (the Arinze posse – I love you guys) our shared laughter, your love, support and belief in me has never wavered – our nightly 'across time zones' WhatsApp banter keeps me sane – would not change you for the world. ♥

My stoic, sacrificial, wise, fiercely protective and supportive **Mummy** – Ifeoma, thank you for being my rock, I love you.

Above all, I want to thank my princesses, **Jade** and **Crystal**. Throughout this journey, you have shown immense maturity, support and have encouraged me in spite of all the time writing this book has taken away from the time I share with you. It has been a long and challenging journey but you never once complained instead, kept spurring me on until I got to the finish line. You have made it so worth it. You are daughters in a million, and as your names show, my precious gifts from God, saying I love you both is an understatement. ♥

Lawrence Arinze Snr: **Daddy**, Thank you for instilling in me from a very young age the joy of reading and writing, self-belief, confidence and a "can-do" resilient attitude. You never believed in impossibilities and now neither do I. *Till we meet again!*

Photo Credit – Front Cover, Victoria Falls Reinvention, Courtesy Kudiwa Nangati – 2016.

And whatever you do, whether in word or deed,
do it all in the name of the Lord Jesus,
giving thanks to God the Father through him.
Colossians 3:17

Thank you!

TABLE OF CONTENTS

The Butterfly's Heart

The heart of the butterfly is strong but meek

The longing for a love that shone but now is gone

And wishing for a time when all had seemed

So straight ahead, in path for you.

A once in a lifetime love you sought

But this was the beginning of the journey you fought.

An adventure for two

While silently learning

Where love is loss, life is gained

From we to me

A chapter's closing

And that was alright for you.

You've felt the pain of journey's end

You've grieved for love and loss

And like a caterpillar you'll descend

Into your cocoon

But you'll ascend.

To Believe, Heal and Live Again

With colours so bold, audacious and beautiful

And a touch of a winters passed

With strength of a Zina warrior

You'll relearn to fly

And confidence a-bloom

You'll soar into the sky

Releasing the past

As once a caterpillar left to its fate

Is now a beautiful butterfly with a future so great

Gliding so fast

Into a life brand new

Overflowing in promises and opportunities

Welcome to the Reinvented YOU!

PROLOGUE

Sitting in traffic with hot tears streaming down my face, it took me a while to realise the lights had changed to green and it was time to move. Amidst the loud horns beeping with impatience behind me, as I continuously replayed this morning's events over and over again in my mind, the pain of the memory was almost enough to finally tip me over the edge.

"A fool at 40 is a fool forever."

This is what my 'wasband' had yelled to me on the morning of my 40th birthday. No surprise party or thoughtful present for this wonderful milestone. No pampering session or heartfelt card. Just humiliation and heartbreak for the umpteenth time. Dejected, I mumbled to God,

"Why, God, Why? Not an atom of respite from the daily tirade of emotional abuse, even on my 40th? How did I get it so terribly wrong? Lord, am I really such a horrible wife?"

I remembered, how the previous night at 3am, I'd placed a heavily soiled diaper in the kitchen bin. It's not something I'd normally do, but it was 3am in the morning and our toddler daughter had decided it was a good way to wake me up. The stench and mess was everywhere, yet my gorgeous daughter just gurgled with glee as we made our way to the bathroom. As I gave her a bath for the umpteenth time and she smiled up into my eyes, I wish I could say I felt an ounce of her joy. Oh boy!

Was I tired? I knew that the refuse collectors were scheduled to come the next morning and I'd already emptied the bathroom bins, so I made a mental note before going back into bed, to lug the diaper filled heavy kitchen bin out early in the morning, the day of my 40th birthday, before I dashed out to work. I left the bin with the nappy in the refuse bag downstairs, by the front door, as a reminder to myself.

Exhausted, I crept back into bed, careful not to disturb my 'wasband'. I drifted back into sleep dreaming of breakfast in bed, 1000 I love you's and wonderful surprises – a new car, a cruise or something special to mark my 40th. I awoke to a surprise alright! An absolutely terrifying, heart-wrenching shock. My 'wasband' had searched for the bin, looking to throw away his left over breakfast, and had found it by the front door. I heard him grumble impatiently to himself, most likely at the inconvenience of having to go downstairs to find the bin. When I heard his scream, I knew he had discovered the diaper. He shouted angrily, his face contorting in rage.

"Zina! How could you be so stupid? Why are you so lazy? Why is the bin by the front door, and why on earth is there a soiled diaper in the kitchen bin?"

Questions, questions, questions, I thought. "Honey," I pleaded, "not today, please not today." I assumed he'd forgotten. Then he struck me. Not physically, but he might as well have because quite frankly the pain he inflicted with his words was so intense, it still stings to think about it many years later. He screeched venomously as our young daughters looked on in bewilderment.

"A fool at 40 is a fool forever!"

This is my story, a story of a reluctant and unplanned single mother of two pre-teen daughters. A story of a woman left broken when her 'wasband' deserted her 10 years ago. A story of a woman left without means to sufficiently support herself, or her two children. Although we lived in a 5-bedroom town house, being alone, I couldn't afford the upkeep when my 'wasband' left.

One year in particular, it was so bad that during the winter months, my young daughters and I lived without proper heating. I just could not afford to heat the entire house as well as feed and clothe the girls. We were reduced to living in the sitting room, heated by a tiny Argos convection heater. We kept warm under several layers of clothing, heavy jogging bottoms, double socks, and duvets. In spite of all of this, the girls and I were happy. My gorgeous amazing children, never once complained. In fact, they often look back on this time fondly, remembering it as snugly fun.

Perhaps unsurprisingly, my 'wasband' still owes me over 10 years of 'unclaimed' CSA support – he has yet to pay a single pound. To be fair, I never once made a claim, too scared

16

to rock the boat, especially since he does pay the mortgage (albeit interest only). I've heard several stories where other women's 'wasband's' stopped paying the mortgage and the family was turned out onto the streets. I guess it's all about trade-offs isn't it?

Yes, he does pay the mortgage for our home, our home that was deceptively bought in his name. My 'wasband' had charmingly convinced me to take out a £15,000 bank loan for the deposit for the house. We had (or so I thought) an understanding that he would remortgage the following year and he would give me the money back to repay the loan. Of course this never happened, and he left me with huge debts to pay.

Aside from being a terrible husband, he is also an absentee father, albeit a loving one; he does phone our daughters regularly and visits from time to time to take them out at unplanned and irregular intervals, but does not seem to turn up on the occasions that mean the most to them, like milestone birthdays, parents' evenings and first day at University. Despite this, admittedly, he does have a somewhat good personal relationship with them, for which I am eternally grateful. Any small relationship is better than none at all, as long as it is a good one.

I had decided a long time ago, that even if I could not save my marriage, I would do all that I could to protect their father/daughter relationship. This hasn't been easy for me and has come at great personal cost, especially from an emotional standpoint, but I strongly believe that this is a sacrifice all mothers should make if they find themselves in a similar position, more so when you have daughters. As a mother, you want to ensure as much as you are able that you raise wholesome and self-confident young women who do not see the need to seek solace in father figures or make other detrimental life choices. I do worry, however, that their relationship with their own father is too remote in that he doesn't really know them or fully understand and appreciate their needs. Yet, I'm still grateful that some kind of relationship exists between them and trust that God will do whatever else may be needed.

Our marriage wasn't a complete disaster; there were good times. My 'wasband' was very charismatic, very handsome, health conscious and incredibly intelligent with a fantastic sense of humour and sense of adventure. He has such an infectious and hearty laugh that one of our daughter's seems to have inherited. Confident and successful, truthfully, he seemed like the perfect catch. He was so charming and gallant; I could not believe my blessings when we first got together.

It was a whirlwind romance; we met in May 1995 in the library. He was studying for his American Medical exams and I was studying for my QLLT (Qualified Lawyers Legal Transfer Test) exams. For me, it was love at first sight. He was charming, infectious and seemed to know what he wanted in life and how he was going to get there. Also, as we were both Born Again Christians, I believed he was a miracle from God.

By March 1996, we were married. It was at this stage that I discovered with a jolt that my 'wasband' had ensnared me. Now we were married, the charm offensive was switched off and my life had changed forever.

Essentially, something was missing; my 'wasband' appeared to be withholding something from me – himself. There was a disconnect; an unexplainable absence, he was there but not there. We would be in the house together, but even a fly on the wall would find it difficult to ascertain that we were man and wife. If truth be told, it would be a complete understatement to say that our marriage was simply 'unhappy' because it was more than that – fraught with control, belittlement, selfishness, emotional abuse, and disconnection.

That notwithstanding, I stayed in the marriage as I felt it was my duty to do so and that it was entirely my fault that my 'wasband' treated me the way he did. Throughout my marriage, I wore a mask; I wore a mask for 14 years. I kept up appearances so I guess most people thought that, yes, we had a few problems like young couples do, but ostensibly, we were a great family with a solid marriage.

Regrettably, my 'wasband' was a total control freak which led to many tantrums and intimidating tirades when he didn't get his way or I attempted to have a voice. It always had to be his way or the highway. I lived in terror and constant bewilderment, but I hid these problems from everyone who cared about me. Instead, I tried to fix things and took the blame with the hope that, if I tried harder, our marriage would get better. It didn't and the state of my marriage was beginning to take its toll, it was slowly eroding my self-confidence and self-esteem, but guess what? I still stayed, still hoping it would get better. It didn't; it got worse. There were beatings at the slightest opportunity, verbal abuse and put-downs as well as systematic emotional abuse by regularly "blanking" me at home. That is, purposely refusing to acknowledge my very presence. Yet, I still stayed.

Zina, this is your lot, suck it up and live with it – God is in control. A wise woman builds her home and a foolish woman with her own hands tears it down, I told myself. This is what kept me going. I did not want to be that foolish woman.

Even in public he would either "blank me" or jokingly belittle me with wise cracks, and people, not knowing what to do, would laugh awkwardly and so would I to save face. Fundamentally, I really believed it was all my fault.

If only I could be a better wife, be more submissive, more pliable, a proper Christian wife.

I just couldn't stop thinking that if I tried even harder, prayed more, never challenged his authority, but instead always agreed with him, our marriage would get better and he would love me more – forever. *After all, I thought many marriages go through teething problems and then get better. Besides, we were Christian's right? And marriage is forever.*

So many memories, where do I start? Permit me to narrate this in the third person as it makes it easier to bear. Here goes.

'Wasband' had an affair with the Polish au pair, she was young, sporty, and they both spoke Polish. To make matters worse, they even went jogging together every evening… "No!" you scream. YES.

Zina, his wife, would often return from a hard day's work to meet both of them chatting cosily on the family dining table, with the children nowhere in sight. She would ask the au pair about the children and the au pair would, with the quiet support of the 'wasband', pointedly ignore her or respond in a belligerent manner. Imagine that! Zina, the woman of the house, undermined and made to feel insignificant in her own home and all in the presence of her then husband – now 'wasband'.

Zina prayed constantly to God to show her what to do and to make everything ok. A month or so later, God answered – she finally sacked the au pair.

How on earth was I going to keep my job and make partner in the law firm I worked at, manage my home and the children now, Zina had fretted "What with a job that took me all over the country and Europe?"

Zina had no choice but to employ another au pair – a 19-year-old Polish girl. *What! Why? Another Polish girl?* This was pre EU and they were fantastic workers, wonderful with the kids and managed the house like clockwork.

Peace reigned again; everything was back to normal at home. Surprisingly, Zina and Agneta, the new au pair, got on like a house on fire. They had an amazingly wonderful relationship. Agneta was neat, hardworking, fun and really engaging. The children absolutely adored her. She was also extremely astute and fiercely loyal – she'd figured out within the first couple of hours in their home that the marriage was stormy. She'd often ask Zina, "What are you doing with such a horrible unappreciative man?" Zina would smile sweetly and say,

"Don't worry, when you grow older you'll understand why it is important as a woman of faith to be submissive no matter what and do all you can to save your marriage".

In the September of that year, five months or so after Agneta started working for the family, Zina had to go away on a weekend business trip to Dublin leaving her 'wasband', daughters and Agneta, the au pair, behind. By the time Zina returned, very late Sunday night, Agneta was gone.

Unbeknownst to her at the time, apparently, it had transpired that her 'wasband' had been making frequent advances towards Agneta and would attempt to strike up disparaging discussions with her in Polish about his wife. Agneta would retort in English that she came to England to perfect her English and that she did not find it appropriate to discuss her boss.

The straw that finally broke the camel's back during that fateful weekend was when he had allegedly been making frequent lewd and suggestive remarks which had culminated in him attempting to fondle her.

Agneta was so devastated; she couldn't sleep a wink that night, so she got up gingerly and called her Australian boyfriend and just broke down on the phone. He understandably flew into such a rage that he got into his car immediately and drove down to the family home to confront Zina's 'wasband'.

Fortunately, on arrival, all he met were the children and an emotional Agneta because 'wasband' was away on call at work. Her boyfriend then insisted strongly that Agneta move out there and then, and so with a lot of reluctance and regret, with tears streaming down her face, Agneta moved out instantly, leaving two very bewildered and emotional children with the neighbour all day until 'wasband' returned from work that evening.

Zina was livid. Even if these allegations were false or exaggerated, how could he be so stupid and arrogant to put himself in this position in the first place? Surely as a professional, he understood the boundaries expected by his profession.

What transpired after that event, Zina thought at the time, was no less than a wonderful miracle, the ingredients fairy tales are made of. 'Wasband' suddenly quite literally became the best husband in the world. He wined and dined Zina, became a tender lover and still spoke to her lovingly the next morning. He constantly supported, affirmed and encouraged her when she was having a challenging time at work – something he had never done before. He also supported her while she was writing her MBA assignments. He even looked after the children so that Zina could have 'ME' time and he bought her thoughtful gifts.

Zina should have smelt a rat, and she is the first to admit it, but she was so elated believing the transformation was an answer to her years of prayer, that she became completely blinkered, so much so that she utterly failed to realise that what her 'wasband' was actually doing was buying her support...and gosh, he needed it in bucket loads!

'Wasband' was counting on Zina's wonderful relationship with Agneta, especially since Agneta and her boyfriend eventually proposed a pay-off. 'Wasband' approached Zina with this proposition to ask for her views.

Asking me for my views, she thought suspiciously. *If he didn't do it why agree to a payoff – Agneta should only get any unpaid salary and nothing more,* she reasoned.

All the same, she asked him yet again, if the allegations were true and he responded with an emphatic NO. Zina decided there and then that her duty as a loving supportive wife was to believe and support her 'wasband' and family through this. Also, she saw how their relationship had changed for the better. Out of this adversity, they had become a stronger and much closer couple. God's grace was indeed shining upon their marriage.

Zina really wanted it to work; she believed they had finally turned a corner and thought their relationship was finally for keeps, so she stayed. This was to last until just before Christmas of that year. Yes! The euphoria of love lasted a mere three months.

Zina had met up with Agneta a long time afterwards because they had become and still are firm friends. She confessed to Zina that at the time, she felt physically sick and violated. Of course 'wasband' had vehemently denied that there was ever any wrong doing so, to a degree, it became his word against Agneta's.

Zina was confused and conflicted. However, with so little evidence she asked herself, was she really prepared to drag her family through this? Zina was at her wit's end, more so since these allegations were extremely serious with the potential of affecting her children and damaging 'wasband's' career, not to talk of his reputation. Yet in the final analysis, it was the potential damage it could do to their children that was of paramount importance. Zina had constant visions of them being teased and bullied at school, becoming moody, depressed, uncommunicative or disruptive and this was a risk Zina, as a mother, was not prepared to take.

Zina decided to stand by her husband with a lot of stern conditions attached. These were around boundaries and expected standards of behaviour around the live-in child care and domestic help. She also used the opportunity to leverage her better treatment and respect by him. It looked like this situation had caused their marriage to turn a corner. Sadly, the fairy tale was short-lived. Once it looked like the storm had blown over, he fled to 'greener' pastures with a new girlfriend – a nurse – under the guise of being on permanent call.

The process was sly and almost undetectable. He proceeded by underhandedly removing Zina from all the joint business accounts and directorships. Zina only noticed when she was out shopping and the business debit card in her name was declined.

He left his wife with nothing but whatever she earned from her solicitor's job as an external fee earner which, to be frank, was fantastic when she was able to work. However, the children were often sick spending weeks on end in hospital, so with no paid holidays or sick pay, having no steady income soon became an incredibly stressful time. Unpaid red bills started building up, but Zina made sure that her children were kept well dressed, warm and never went hungry.

Zina, continued to wear her mask, keeping up appearances as best she could despite the disturbing incidences of emotional abuse and intolerable unreasonable behaviour she experienced at the hands of her 'wasband'.

Even with all this, it would be unfair to convey that the 'wasband' was all wrong and Zina was all right. In fact, there is the temptation to continue with further harrowing stories of emotional misuse and abuse and there are many – but then the whole point of this book would be negated. In any event, there are always two sides of every story. If 'wasband' was so bad, why did Zina marry him? Again, if 'wasband' were asked today to give his own side of the story, it is almost a guarantee that Zina would definitely not come out smelling of roses.

INTRODUCTION

"There are things that we don't want to happen
but have to Accept,
Things we don't want to know
but have to Learn,
And people we can't live without
but have to Let Go".
~ Author Unknown

If you are reading this book, I must stress that the point is not yet another "I married a monster" blame game book, but rather it is a book of hope.

If you have suffered from a traumatic divorce or relationship breakdown, I want you to know there is hope, yes! There is hope. Regardless of the circumstances, the 'who' or 'what' was at fault, ditch the blame game; now it is all about you. Yes, you. You can move on to a better life. I have and I repeat, so can you!

The question is, do you want to grow through divorce or just go through it? This is the fundamental question Edward Tauber and Jim Smoke (divorce recovery experts and counsellors), drawing on their 30 years of experience, ask in their bestselling book *Divorce: Healing and Moving On: 10 Step Process* proven successful with thousands of divorced people in over thirty years of divorce recovery workshops. They advised that there is a major difference between growing through your divorce as opposed to just going through it.

In this amazing book, Edward M Tauber and Jim Smoke invite us to examine what it takes to grow through divorce.

Here are some synonyms provided for the word *grow* taken from a number of dictionaries:

To Grow:

- Advance – to move forward, not be stuck
- Branch out – to expand beyond the life you have
- Develop – to realise potentialities
- Expand – to increase your scope of activities

- Flourish – to thrive, prosper
- Mature – to mentally develop
- Show life – to function, not be dead inside
- Spring up – to move out of one place to another
- Stretch – to reach or extend into untried areas

I would imagine that, like I did when I first discovered this amazing resource in 2009, you would want this for yourself too. That is, to grow after divorce, to be empowered to heal, to advance, expand your possibilities, tap into your opportunities, realise your untapped potentialities, discover how to fully function again, move out of the old dead place and stretch yourself to flourish; achieve a new, fulfilling, reinvented, better and bigger life. *A Believe and Live Again* life! This is what good looks like growing through divorce.

Here's the thing; if you are recently divorced or in the process of getting a divorce, to achieve all of this may seem almost impossible. You are probably asking yourself the question where do you start? I will put this question another way:

What does it look like for people who just go through their divorce rather than grow through it?

Edward Tauber and Jim Smoke provided some glaring indications that characterise one who has opted to just go through divorce rather than grow through it:

- You stay stuck, frozen, and unable to act
- You remain in denial that you are divorced
- You remain bitter, angry, and remorseful
- You are steeped in guilt over 'your failure'
- You perpetually play the 'if only' game – If only I had done this or that or been this or that, he/she wouldn't have left
- You obsess about why your former spouse acted as he/she did
- You encourage your friends to choose sides against your ex
- You continue to fight with your ex

- ♥ You allow your ex to control you or you try to control your ex

- ♥ You think about the divorce 24/7

- ♥ You repeat your divorce story to anyone who will listen

- ♥ You blame your ex for all your problems

- ♥ You put your children in the middle of battles with your ex

- ♥ You encourage your children to spy on your ex

- ♥ You stay vengeful toward your ex, threatening, scheming

- ♥ You suffer declining emotional and physical health

- ♥ You search for someone to rescue you from your problems

- ♥ You remarry quickly to cover up your pain

Although these are typical feelings you could go through and might be going through right now, I have decided to lift these very negative characteristics directly from *Divorce: Healing and Moving On* because I think it would be a travesty if I didn't tell you how your potential current thoughts and actions can potentially hinder your divorce recovery or relationship breakup bounce-back process in a very detrimental way. My sole purpose is to shock as you go down the list; to shock you into taking positive rebuilding action so that you can **REINVENT YOU and Believe, Heal and Live Again!**

When I think back to my own divorce experience, what happened as a consequence, to my mind, was nothing short of a miracle. For some strange reason, I started to research and devour everything I could lay my hands on regarding the subject of improving and rebuilding my life after divorce.

What I discovered completely changed my life!

I am so grateful to God, for my personal divorce recovery journey, harrowing as it may have been, because through it, I have been able to rediscover and live my passion and purpose, helping women all over the world to rapidly move past the grief of divorce and abuse to positively impact lives for the better all over the world. It is my sincere hope that as you go through the following chapters, teeming with the advice and guidance gathered from a plethora of experts the world over in the field of divorce recovery coaching, counselling and mental health as well as the golden nuggets from my own personal experience, you too will be in a position to regain your feminine power, rediscover your passion and purpose and finally Believe, Heal and Live Again.

You might be asking, "What qualifies Zina to write a Divorce Recovery book?"

Let's deal with that now before we get too far. What qualifies me is that I get it, I have been there. I have been rock bottom and back, emotionally, physically, spiritually and even financially. I was once as far low down as I ever want to be again. Apart from that, I am a Lawyer, an IT Project Management Consultant, Certified Divorce Recovery Coach, and a Born Again Woman of God, so all bases are covered professionally, spiritually and emotionally. But I have to say that it was through the emotional journey that miraculously, through the grace and strength of God, that I was able to turn my life around, climbing back up from the trauma, the grief and devastation that is divorce by applying many of the ideas and strategies you will find in this book.

This is a simple book jam-packed to the brim with anecdotes, my personal journal entries, wry humour, practical strategies, tools as well as specific divorce-coaching best practice techniques I use with clients from across the globe in my divorce recovery coaching service to achieve desired results. Also included, as a special bonus, are experiential tips from my personal journey, exercises to help you along and a chapter especially dedicated to dealing with how to avoid the typical mistakes people make in divorce so as not to end up having a huge negative impact on your future or cause you to make unnecessary financial errors. This is a book that anyone who is divorcing, divorced, separated or been affected by a relationship breakdown will find extremely useful.

How did I do it? In this book, I share the secrets of my incredible journey by bringing you a collection of my learning, advice, valuable information and practical steps on how I moved from "we to me", rebuilt my life and rediscovered my passion and purpose after my divorce. And guess what? You can too. I leave absolutely nothing out. The book comprises of the Prologue, Introduction, Epilogue and 21 Chapters spread over 8 key themes in order to help you navigate your REINVENT YOU! divorce recovery journey from "WE" to "ME" as smoothly and as swiftly as possible.

There are many resources out there postulating steps, processes, etc. for post-divorce recovery and although it is good to have structure, you will find in this book, that more often than not the steps are not linear or chronological. I mean, it is life we are talking about and as much as many of us would want our lives to follow our best laid plans, life, including divorce, does not. So this book, although it is broken down into themes, chapters and sub chapters and in some places, steps, etc., is more for structure as opposed to a prescriptive process for divorce recovery. This is because your journey will be different and you will need to find and follow your journey intuitively. There's no easy five-step plan to quickly get over the deep wounding of a divorce. But there are steps you can take to move gradually toward healing in whatever order you are comfortable with. This is what this book seeks to achieve. My guarantee is as you read and go through this book you can go from wherever you are in your life now at this moment in time in terms of healing, rebuilding and recovery to soaring up into a Believe and Live Again life that is truly the life of your dreams.

Today, I often pinch myself and marvel at the wonderful life I am living. I am exceptionally grateful to God every day for the way He has restored me and turned my life around. I am in total awe of how he has consistently favoured me and the amazing daughters He has given me. I am doing what I love with the five talents God has graced me with. I am having a positive transformational effect on the lives of so many across the globe. I look forward with anticipation, excitement and enthusiasm to each new dawn seeking out fresh opportunities and platforms to bless, inspire and heal others – like that professional woman, that female entrepreneur, that abuse victim, that woman of faith – of the pain and stigma associated with a relationship breakdown. However, above all, I have a peace that I never dreamed possible, I am living my purpose, making a contribution to this world that is 100% uniquely mine. I want you to believe and understand that, in spite of your journey, your life has a purpose too. Don't let the journey get in the way of the purpose.

Please don't just read it, apply it

Please don't just read this book; use it, devour it and apply it. Take from it what is relevant and what you need to make your life everything you hope it can be. Do it now! Because you are worth it, do it now! Because you deserve it, do it now! Because your family deserves the best life possible for them but most importantly – do it now! Because you have only one life. This is your life, it is your sole responsibility to give it your best shot because there are no rinse and repeats.

Making the most out of this book

First off, if you don't already have one, invest in a journal. Those of you who are familiar with my work, webinars and videos would know that journaling is something I absolutely believe in. It has been said that a life worth living is a life worth recording. Your journal does not need to be elaborate. You can go to your local Wilkos and pick up a basic journal at a very reasonable price or you could go for a more up market one that is vibrant, warm, comforting, exciting, colourful, and elaborately designed. I am partial to Paperchase, so most of my journals come from there. A simple spiral notebook works fine. The point is to go free hand, writing in a physical journal rather than onto your mobile device or PC. It is like keeping a diary; your journal serves as a safe confidential place to record your thoughts, ideas, feelings, observations and plans. It is a safe haven to record your dreams, visions and goals.

You can decide how frequently you want to write in it but the secret is consistency.

I have found through my own journaling habits that one of the greatest benefits has been having the ability to go back through the years, reading my entries, seeing how far I have come and discovering how many dreams have either come true or have been reframed into even bigger and better dreams. All through this book, you will find exercises; I am confident that you will get the greatest value if you write down these exercises in your journal and make the effort to actually do them. As I said earlier, these strategies and tips work, but only with the proviso that you use and do them.

My suggestion would be to read the entire book then go back and invest some quality time in doing the exercises and applying the strategies. Please don't just take what I have written on blind faith. Be like the Berean Christians in the Bible.

And the people of Berea were more open-minded than those in Thessalonica, and they listened eagerly to Paul's message. They searched the Scriptures day after day to see if Paul and Silas were teaching the truth. Acts 17:11

Make every effort. Test the principles, and work with the ideas. If you happen to find something that is not congruent to your beliefs, my advice would be to just use what works for you and your reality.

Now sit tight and put on your seat belts as you embark upon a journey that you will find becomes so incredibly inspiring, powerful and exciting. Enjoy your journey – Believe and Live Again!

My intention for this book is not to be another "I was married to a monster" book, even if that were to be true, but rather to be a catalyst for hope and new beginnings for you. You can decide to take advantage of the story shared in this prologue and read further into this book so as to draw from the tips, guidance and advice provided.

Many of the tips and guidance are drawn from my personal experience and from my liaisons over the years with other mentors, divorce recovery coaches, and other relationship experts to help you begin to live the life you deserve.

You can honestly start from today to stop defining yourself as that poor victim, the hard done-by divorcee, that 'common law' wife or living together partner' who never got the ring and got dumped after 15 years, but instead see yourself as the hugely successful, strong professional woman or woman of faith that you are; not a victim but a Victoria.

You could be a mother or not, a grandmother or a sister, a friend or colleague, a Born Again Christian or not, it doesn't matter. Just as the pain is real, so is my message. I am here to tell you that you are an indomitable, elegant and amazing woman. To even come this far by picking up this book, I applaud and celebrate you

Admittedly, my marriage did break down, but I have ended up a stronger and better woman for it, a woman of substance, a grown-up who has learnt the lessons I needed to learn from my experiences and made the life changes I needed to make to become a better version of me.

Consequently, I am committed to helping women just like me come out victoriously at the other end. I am passionate about not allowing you to be stuck in the past with the mind-set that you married Mr. Wrong and therefore will be a victim forever. I firmly believe that there are so many women out there that need to hear this message and tangibly see that there is hope, yes hope, in your future more glorious than your past. I guarantee that, like me, you can recover completely from the trauma, grief and stigma of divorce or a long term relationship break up with your significant other. You can transition from "we" to "me" so that you do not just survive after divorce but you thrive – perhaps even find love again – and transition back from "me" to "we". Now that would be something, wouldn't it? If that is what you desire. It is never too late.

Transitioning from "we" to "me" to a new life as a "whole" person without the presence of your ex-spouse is often a painstakingly slow process that can lead to feelings of sadness, low self-esteem and depression along with unanticipated legal and financial struggles, but if I can do it, so can you.

On your part, there is only one condition – you, my sister, have to want to Believe and Live Again. You have to want to live a reignited life full of passion and purpose. The world is waiting for you to leave your mark, so make your life count now.

Enjoy your REINVENT YOU Journey as you, too, move smoothly from "we" to "me" by Believing, Healing and Living Again. Give yourself the permission to be bold and audacious as you get back on track, rewrite your story and rediscover your purpose.

Whether you are just at the beginning of your journey or shifting directions as a result of your journey or just sick and tired of being sick and tired and want your life to sing a new song, this book will ensure you get to your new exciting appointment with destiny.

Trust the process, Be self-compassionate and Trust You.

Zina ♥♪

AND SO THE TALE BEGINS...

27th March 2006

Hiya Journie,

It's me again. I have always loved talking to you ever since I could write. I can still remember when you were just my little purple "Dear Diary" with the bronze lock on it and I used to share my most intimate thoughts - why am I so tall and every other 6-year-old in class is so small - maybe I'll get as tall as the sky! Why doesn't mummy believe me when I say my "TUFF" shoes are tight again after two weeks - humph! Then I became a teenager and I got you - my big black leather diary and a gold signet ring from Daddy for Christmas, but you had no key. I quickly learnt Backslang and poured out my heart in code to stop Mummy from knowing my secrets.

At 18, I got my first journal - lovely girly one with flowers and the sun setting into the horizon and suddenly 'Dear Diary' sounded lame so I renamed you to 'Journie' and you have been that ever since; my faithful and loyal friend; together we have gone through all my highs and lows. You have never once given me a reason not to trust you.

Today is the worst day of my life, I got a letter in the post from a firm of solicitors - my husband is asking for a divorce...

Unless this is your reality and it has happened to you, you cannot even begin to understand or imagine the impact it will have on your life.

I remember it as clear as rain, as if it were yesterday. The huge sense of failure and regret; the intense emotional upheaval; the disillusionment and overwhelming pain I felt when my marriage finally broke down irretrievably. It took me a while to recover and even then I used to have flashbacks of the life we shared. It wasn't a good marriage, but I had become adept at keeping up appearances and somehow I believed the hype myself, so much so that I convinced myself it was better to be in an abusive, unhappy marriage than be divorced. To use a phrase many of us church people use: "that was a lie from the pit of hell."

I tried to carry on as normal, keeping up appearances, but inwardly my life was closed firmly shut to everyone on the outside world. I decided, I would never let anyone in, I would never allow myself to fall in love again and I would never trust.

Consequently, I found that:

♥ Although I had a successful career, I was still struggling to move forward with my life after divorce.

♥ I often felt overwhelmed, robotic and unable to give myself the nurturing self-care I so desperately needed and deserved.

♥ I became tired of not living as my authentic self; I lost my spark.

Friends and colleagues saw my new persona as aloof. Many who only got to meet me after my divorce found me snobbish and stand-offish. I knew that my dispassionate professional persona was a farce, miles away from the real me who was hurting inside. I wore a mask in church, at work and even at home, covering up my fear, anxieties and vulnerabilities. Each day, at work in particular, I found myself being present in body only. Fortunately, at the time, I was able to keep all the balls in the air and keeping up appearances became an art form, but in reality I was scared, anxious and worried that one day I would make a drastic and costly mistake, drop my aloof guard that would cost me my job, the organisation's bottom line and my reputation.

28th March 2006

Dear Journie,

I feel so lost, confused, unsure, disoriented, perplexed, downright bewildered, and alone. How can this happen to me? How can this happen to us? Where is God? I feel as if I have failed him, I am such a failure.

God, I am so sorry, please forgive me. How can I sort this out? What will happen to the girls? Will he take them away? Am I such a terrible wife and a horrible Christian? Lord, I love you, Jesus do you really love me? I just can't stop crying. I must wipe my eyes, I can't let the girls see and know how incredibly sad I am. God please help me, please help us.................

Reading this back now, I can't believe I went through so much anguish. I do remember often feeling lost, confused, unsure, disoriented, perplexed, downright bewildered and alone after the breakdown. I had so many people around me, especially while at church, but they didn't really understand or even want to know what I was going through. I could see the silent starts, the whispers, they knew I was bad news as a Christian woman, scarlet, tainted and so alone, smothered and suffocating under the stigma of divorce. I was so wrapped up in the divorce trauma I was going through at the time, I really believed that I was the only one.

If you are going through a similar situation, please be encouraged, you are not alone. You might feel that way; I get that because I thought I was alone too, but there is not room for shame, for guilt or for self-imposed stigma.

Take a look at stats, or as Gil Grissom would say in CSI, "follow the evidence" and you will discover, just like I did, that it tells us a different story; divorce is rife in the UK and in our global society:

Divorces in the US and the UK

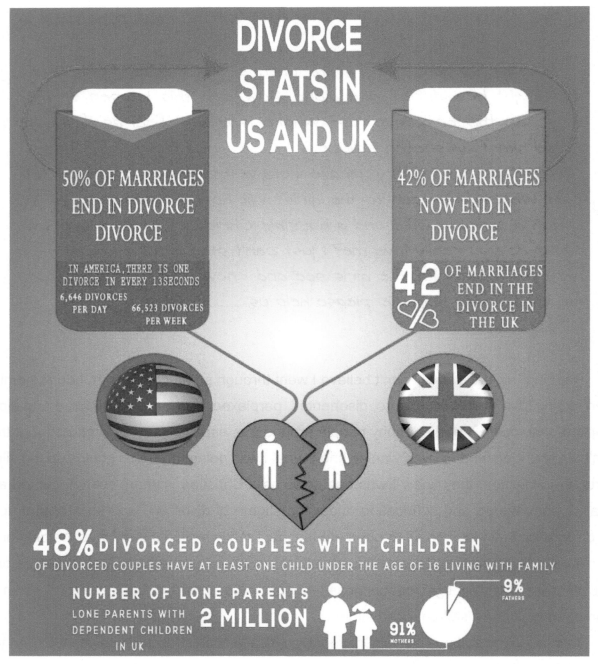

---

1   Divorce statistics in USA and UK

Is Divorce Really That Common?

In the United States alone, there are about one divorce every 13 seconds.

- ♥ The average length of a first marriage is just 8 years.
- ♥ 41% of first marriages end in divorce
- ♥ 50% of marriages in general end in divorce.

Whether you are a Christian or not, the stats have said it all – divorce appears to be rising. There are a lot of disillusioned hurting people all over the world wondering how on earth their marriages fell apart and how they will ever recover, heal or even love or be loved again. No matter what side of the fence you sit on, whether you are judgmental or empathetic, if you are not or have not gone through the pain and grief of divorce or a relationship breakdown, you have no idea how debilitating this can be. Anyone going through this emotional and legal rollercoaster needs all the help and reassurance they can get. Maybe this is you right now and as you are reading this, tears are welling up or maybe you are feeling a whole plethora of emotions, anger and regret being right at the top. Whatever you may be feeling, I get it. I am sharing this because, firstly, as a divorced professional woman, a serial entrepreneur, a mum and a woman of faith, as well as in my capacity as a certified divorce recovery coach, a lawyer, and as a minister of the gospel, I have had the humbling opportunity to observe, mentor, coach and counsel so many women the world over who have experienced similar scenarios to the ones I experienced; women who have taken longer than anticipated to recover from the aftermath of divorce or a relationship breakdown for the simple reason that they were not aware that there are resources and help available or were unwilling to use them due to shame, guilt or fear.

Note of Caution

No two divorces or relationship break ups for that matter are the same. For this reason, it is incredibly difficult to write a book giving sweeping 'one size fit all' divorce advice because quite frankly one size does not and cannot fit all. In addition, I would be running the risk of readers thinking, *how does Zina know? I'm a man and she's a woman,* or *"she didn't get*

divorced because her husband committed adultery," or *she has no clue whatsoever how it feels to have your Christian wife kick you out* or *she just won't understand what I'm feeling.*

And you would be absolutely 100% correct, it would be insensitive to argue otherwise, because the honest fact is that I do not know or understand how every divorced person feels in every situation. However, what I do know and can tell you is that there are lots of feelings that are common. This book therefore offers divorce recovery advice based on the way many divorced people, including me, felt or feel, from the moment their ex-spouse said, "I want a divorce," (or they said it to their spouse.) This book was also written to help you navigate the nuts and bolts of your emotions and feelings, help you define your amazing new life by developing new personal goals, getting organised and discovering the resources you need to rewrite your own story after divorce enabling you to take action so that you believe and live in your dreams and in YOU. Perhaps you have unprocessed or residual feelings of bitterness, shame, guilt, unforgiveness, anger, sadness, rejection, disappointment, blame, or regret in separating from someone you once loved and this is preventing you from healing your heart and moving on after divorce.

Or maybe:

- ♥ You find yourself drowning in sorrow and confusion.
- ♥ You lay in bed at night crying wondering what went wrong in your marriage and fretting how you will cope financially as you downgrade from a "we" to "me" in terms of joint to single person income.
- ♥ You constantly question what you could have done to arrive at a different outcome.
- ♥ You may even feel as though gathering the courage to date someone new and to eventually find love again is impossible. "What! After everything I've been through?"
- ♥ You know you are getting stronger and really want to move on, get your groove back, but it's hard for you to trust and risk getting hurt again. You may even find it downright frightening to put yourself back out there, you are scared of meeting another Mr. Wrong or maybe you simply don't know how.

- ♥ You are afraid of what the future holds. Do you feel as if you are on a permanent emotional rollercoaster and you can't get off?

- ♥ You feel like you've gotten over your divorce or relationship breakdown to a certain point, but you are still unsure what this really means and if you have really recovered.

- ♥ Perhaps you often wonder how your life will pan out after the trauma of divorce or relationship breakdown. I did.

To be honest, I did not just wonder, I agonised, spending many a day and night just crying in anguish and regret, my face buried into serial Costco-sized tubs of ice cream, watching reruns of *Love Story* and *When Harry Met Sally* while asking myself 'why did my marriage fail? What did I do wrong? And what could I have done differently?'

Being a successful lawyer and then becoming an accomplished Project Management Consultant to multinational organisations and governmental bodies, I thought I had hit the

41

big time as I travelled the world for work. I was married to a doctor and we had two young beautiful children in quick succession. As far as I was concerned, my most challenging life experience (or so I thought) was managing my home, childcare, career, and achieving the ever elusive work-life balance. My role model was the Proverbs 31 wife and my personal mantra was Proverbs 14:1

"…a wise woman builds her house
but with her own hands;
the foolish one tears hers down".

A Wife of Noble Character – Proverbs 31:10 – 31(NLT)

10 [b] Who can find a virtuous and capable wife?
She is more precious than rubies.

11 Her husband can trust her,
and she will greatly enrich his life.

12 She brings him good, not harm,
all the days of her life.

13 She finds wool and flax
and busily spins it.

14 She is like a merchant's ship,
bringing her food from afar.

15 She gets up before dawn to prepare breakfast for her household
and plan the day's work for her servant girls.

16 She goes to inspect a field and buys it;
with her earnings she plants a vineyard.

17   She is energetic and strong,
a hard worker.

18   She makes sure her dealings are profitable;
her lamp burns late into the night.

19   Her hands are busy spinning thread,
her fingers twisting fiber.

20   She extends a helping hand to the poor
and opens her arms to the needy.

21   She has no fear of winter for her household,
for everyone has warm[c] clothes.

22   She makes her own bedspreads.
She dresses in fine linen and purple gowns.

23   Her husband is well known at the city gates,
where he sits with the other civic leaders.

24   She makes belted linen garments
and sashes to sell to the merchants.

25   She is clothed with strength and dignity,
and she laughs without fear of the future.

26   When she speaks, her words are wise,
and she gives instructions with kindness.

27   She carefully watches everything in her household
and suffers nothing from laziness.

28   Her children stand and bless her.
Her husband praises her:

29 "There are many virtuous and capable women in the world,
    but you surpass them all!"

30 Charm is deceptive, and beauty does not last;
    but a woman who fears the Lord will be greatly praised.

31 Reward her for all she has done.
    Let her deeds publicly declare her praise.

I was quite clear in my mind about the roles played in a Christian marriage and each day I was working towards fulfilling my role as a wife as I believed God intended, using Proverbs 31 as my blue print... then BANG! Divorce came along. There is no doubt that divorce can be difficult and one of the most difficult aspects is finding your passion, your purpose and rebuilding your life afterwards.

After a very emotionally and physically abusive marriage resulting in a difficult divorce, I often thought to myself, *I can do this for crying out loud! I'm not the first to get divorced, and besides my strength of character and lively disposition will carry me through and things will be fine.* I kept telling myself the usual clichés. 'After all, how hard could it be?' 'Life happens, I am a tough cookie.' 'Zina get on with it.'

As it turned out and I soon admitted to myself, I was the exact opposite; tough cookie? Cookie dough more like! Hard on the outside and complete goo on the inside.

As hard as I tried, I just could not seem to get on with my life. I kept up appearances, but in fact, quite annoyingly to me, even after my divorce, I just couldn't stop crying. The slightest memory, film or observation would set me off. If I was at work, I would immediately run to the ladies – thinking back I am sure my colleagues must have thought that I was a Tena Lady who may have had a leaking bladder condition or something, what with the way I kept dashing to the "ladies" in a fraction of a second like Usain Bolt.

I noticed many a time the very sly quick looks that my female colleagues would make towards my chair, peering, searching like Lieutenant Colombo on the seating area for tell-tale wet patches. Funny now, especially because they didn't realise I could see them, but not funny then as I couldn't really express what I was going through for fear of losing my job, of ruining my emotional credibility and my work reputation. I had no choice but to keep on my mask. At my level of seniority, it was completely unheard off and unacceptable to show your vulnerability in the work place in that way.

At times, I would have to park my car on a slip road or hard shoulder or even in the car park just to have a good cry.

I was lost; my positive sense of self was all but depleted, and my feminine power all but disappeared. I just wanted my life back, I wanted the tears to stop flooding, but I didn't know where to begin. For me, no matter how traumatic or challenging some of my life experiences may have turned out, it has always been about how to turn a seemingly negative experience into a positive outcome.

It is for this reason, that as a result of my own harrowing experience in the work place, I developed the *Believe and Live Again Signature Coaching Programme from "We" to "Me" Divorce "Bounce Back" Recovery Programme.* This is an intensive 90-day coaching programme promising rapid and effective results, developed and designed with you in mind; the busy female professional, business woman, female entrepreneur or woman of faith who, like I once did, feels constrained to wear a mask in order to hide her vulnerabilities and maintain an appearance of strength and focus in the professional world, market place or ministry in which she finds herself.

During my time, I had no one I could really turn to who understood what I was going through, therefore through this programme, I seek to help women who are at the top of their game, women like you and me, not to fear or suffer reprisals from work, business or ministry so that you are able to navigate the divorce recovery journey as smoothly and as quickly as possible without blame or shame. Quite frankly, I have worn your shoes whether they be high heeled stilettos, flats or wedge heeled sandals and I get it. No matter what shoes we wear, it is important to remember that we can be in control of the direction our life is to take after a break down or divorce.

20th April 2006
Divorce Petition Arrives

Dear Journie,

The divorce papers came in the post today and it is just not true, which is very poignant - today is supposed to be our wedding anniversary.

I am reading these papers; there are just too many lies. My husband stated that we had been living apart and have not slept together for just over two years but that is just not true. We celebrated princess number 1's 7th birthday and threw a massive party for her last year March. I know what the law says. He needs my consent to get this divorce. I just can't deal with this right now.

I am sure if I wake up it will all be a dream. I am not signing away my marriage, I will not give my consent because God hates divorce.

You know what, Journie, I am going to go straight to my lawyer and file a counter petition refusing the divorce but showing that the marriage has irretrievably broken down on account of his adultery with his numerous affairs and unreasonable behaviour. But then I guess the children will get to know all the bad stuff he had been doing with other women; no that wouldn't be good for the family and definitely not good for them. I don't want them to hate their daddy or even hate me for telling the court.

No, I can't deal with this, I am not consenting to this divorce petition. God will be so upset with me.

Dear God, my heart is so heavy, I don't want to face a divorce, I don't want a divorce, but he is so horrible to me, I am always so sad and feel not only alone, but such a failure in my marriage. Lord, can you hear me?

Heavenly Father when we said "I do to each other, I never ever thought in my wildest dreams I would be divorced. Heavenly Father, I am so so sorry, please forgive me - I was sure that You had brought us together and now my whole life seems to be shattered into a million tiny pieces - and we are more like strangers than husband and wife.

Dear God, I am really at my wit's end, please strengthen me, I never believed this would happen. I am so sad. Will I ever find happiness again? Will there ever be an end to the intense pain that I feel deep down in my heart? I feel so lost, draw me closer to you. Father, I really don't think I can face him or the judge in court. Help me not to be drawn into any hostility, Father, please take control, Holy Spirit calm my heart, and cause me not to be ashamed.

Lord look after me and the girls, help me make the right decisions.

Thank You Father for your faithfulness. I know nothing is impossible for You and I have to trust you in this. You always do what You say You will do and will get me through this storm because Your plans for my future are good. I can't see it because of the pain, but I know You can. Father God, as it unfolds, lead me in this journey, In Jesus Name I pray, Amen

24th March 2009
Decree Nisi

Dear Journie,

The decree nisi got awarded today, imagine that! An order by a court of law stating the date on which my marriage will end unless a good reason not to grant a divorce is produced. I wish I can find a good reason, I don't want my marriage to end.

I feel so empty. How did we get here? I know that by law in six weeks and one day we could finally be divorced. I feel really sad. I feel sad because in six weeks and one day, he can apply for the decree absolute and it is unlikely that my marriage will be back on track before that date.

I feel so ashamed. God hates divorce but I have just gone ahead and let it happen. Maybe I could have changed his mind, been a better wife, and been more submissive to his control. The Bible says, "a wise woman builds her house". Could I have been wiser? Could I have prevented this? Maybe it is my entire fault, I made him hate me, hit me, berate me, control me. Should I really be a Christian, do I deserve God? I have failed my family, my husband, my daughters, my church, and my God.

God, help me I pray. I really have tried to be a good wife for many years and to be the wife he wanted - but things just kept going from bad to worse. When he gives me the silent treatment and becomes so hateful I just don't know what to do. Perhaps this is your will for us. Protect me and the children I pray,

Why do I feel so ashamed?

With hindsight, I can say I was ashamed of my new status – I don't really understand why. My marriage was bad from the get go, the signs and red flags were very apparent even before we got married, but I was blinkered and engulfed in rose tinted love. I am ever the romantic and always believed that marriage was forever, that you stuck at it no matter what. We effectively lived apart from 2005, but somehow I never believed we would ever get divorced. But my marriage was stripping me daily of my self-confidence and bubbly effervescent personality. Yet, I was in denial as I rapidly morphed into someone I barely recognised.

Negative self-talk set in

"I was always the life and soul of every gathering, but couldn't manage to be the life and soul of my spouse."

"Zina, if you are that great at work why couldn't you be that great in your marriage?"

Yes, I blamed myself, completely forgetting that there are always two people in a relationship. I subconsciously took full responsibility for the end of my marriage, for everything.

In my head, I had failed my family, let down my church and disappointed my God. With these unfounded, unreasonable and negative limiting beliefs, I began to isolate myself from friends and family and almost stopped going to church altogether. I felt as if I needed to avoid going anywhere: shopping, work, school runs, doctor's surgery, parties, the list was endless, just to avoid running into anyone who would say, "Oh, hello, Zina. I haven't seen you in yonks. How's your husband?" A simple question, you may think, but this would literally make me want to curl up, die and disappear into nothingness.

My unshakeable faith in God was and will always be my anchor; I suddenly realised my faith was being attacked. To be honest, it really wasn't all that sudden of a realisation, but more of a slow "dawning upon". The thing is, I had lost my marriage but I was not about to lose my faith or my praise. It was at that point I knew I had to do something. I prayed and I remember quite clearly as if it was today, the scripture I felt led to read:

For the LORD gives wisdom;
From His mouth come knowledge
and understanding. Proverbs 2:6.

I found it quite incomprehensible; more so since it was not one of the portions of scripture I was familiar with, regularly referred to or readily remembered. Truth be told, during this period of my life, very little scripture came easily to my mind. I couldn't pray like I used to, but because I love music, I listened to a lot of Gospel as well as Praise and Worship songs on the loop.

If you are reading this and you identify as a Christian who is going through a divorce, never ever underestimate the power of praise and worship. If you recall, 2nd Chronicles 20:21:

"King Jehoshaphat appointed men
to sing to the Lord and to praise him
for the splendour of his holiness as
they went out at the head of the army."

Take it from me, I know, when you go through a divorce, you are in a battle that shakes the foundation of your faith. Get out your full armour of God and face that battle armed with the power of praise and worship. I was confused, sad, emotionally exhausted and lonely, but somehow, once I had put my daughters to bed, I would often place my Bible on my chest and fall asleep to praise and worship music. Many nights it was the only way I could sleep.

Ask God to let good come from your pain and suffering. Ask Him for a miracle and then hang on. You are about to embark on the adventure of a lifetime. God delights in using for good what was meant for evil. He did it for me and guess what? He can do it for you.

TBN satellite channel became my close companion. I knew, somehow in the deep recesses of my mind and soul, that even if I was ashamed of myself and felt unlovable, God loved me and was still in control. Three of my favourite songs of all time, which I would say really helped me during my darkest hours, were I *Never Lost My Praise* by The Brooklyn Tabernacle Choir, *I Just Can't Give Up Now* by Mary Mary and *My Life Is In Your Hands* by Kirk Franklin, which I played on the loop in the car, in the house and anywhere I could and when I couldn't play or sing them out loud, I would resort to humming them under my breath. I still do that now so many years later in a much happier state. I guess good habits are good to keep.

I want to take this moment to share these with you here; I hope it offers you the same solace, peace of mind and strength that I received whilst listening.

I Never Lost My Praise

Tremaine Hawkins (2007)
Brooklyn Tabernacle Choir (2008)

Solo 1

I've lost some good friends along life's way
Some loved ones departed in Heaven to stay

But thank God I didn't lose everything
I've lost faith in people who said they care
In the time of my crisis they were never there
But in my disappointment in my season of pain
One thing never wavered one thing never changed
I never lost my hope
I never lost my joy
I never lost my faith
But most of all I never lost my praise

CHOIR

My praise, still here, my praise still — here

Solo 2

I've let some blessings slip away
When I lost my focus and went astray
But thank God I didn't lose everything
I've lost possessions that was so dear
And I've lost some battles by walking in fear
But in the midst of my struggle, in the season of pain
One thing never wavered, one thing never changed

I never lost my hope
I never lost my joy
I never lost my faith
But most of all I never lost my praise

 **Can't Give Up Now**

Mary Mary (2000)

There will be mountains that I will have to climb
And there will be battles that I will have to fight
But victory or defeat, it's up to me to decide
But how can I expect to win if I never try.

I just can't give up now
I've come too far from where I started from
Nobody told me the road would be easy
And I don't believe he brought me this far to leave me

Never said there wouldn't be trials
Never said I wouldn't fall
Never said that everything would go the way I want it to go
But when my back is against the wall
And I feel all hope is gone,
I'll just lift my head up to the sky
And say help me to be strong

I just can't give up now
I've come too far from where I started from
Nobody told me the road would be easy
And I don't believe he brought me this far to leave me
No you didn't bring me out here to leave me lonely
Even when I can't see clearly
I know that you are with me (so I can't)
I just can't give up now
I've come too far from where I started from
Nobody told me the road would be easy
And I don't believe he brought me this far to leave me

My Life Is In Your Hands

Kirk Franklin (1997)

You don't have to worry
And don't you be afraid
Joy comes in the morning
Troubles they don't last always
For there's a friend named Jesus
Who will wipe your tears away
And if your heart is broken
Just lift your hands and say

CHORUS
Oh! I know that I can make it
I know that I can stand
No matter what may come my way
My life is in your hands
You don't have to worry
And don't you be afraid
Joy comes in the morning
Troubles they don't last always
For there's a friend named Jesus
Who will wipe your tears away
And if your heart is broken
Just lift your hands and say

CHORUS
Oh! I know that I can make it
I know that I can stand
No matter what may come my way
My life is in your hands

54

CHORUS II

With Jesus I can take it
With Him I know I can stand
No matter what may come my way
My life is in your hands

So when your tests and trials
They seem to get you down
And all your friends and loved ones
Are nowhere to be found
Remember there's a friend named Jesus
Who will wipe your tears away
And if you heart is broken
Just lift your hands and say

CHORUS

Oh! I know that I can make it
I know that I can stand
No matter what may come my way
My life is in your hands

Fairy Tale

Anita Baker (1990)

I can remember stories,
those things my mother said
She told me fairy tales, before I went to bed
She spoke of happy endings, then tucked me in real tight
She turned my night light on, and kissed my face good night

My mind would fill with visions, of perfect paradise
She told me everything, she said he'd be so nice
He'd ride up on his horse and, take me away one night
I'd be so happy with him, we'd ride clean out of sight
She never said that we would, curse, cry and scream and lie
She never said that maybe, someday he'd say goodbye

The story ends, as stories do
Reality steps into view
No longer living life in paradise – of fairy tales – uh
No, uh – huh – mmm – mmm
She spoke about happy endings, of stories not like this
She said…

Chapter 1.

TAKING IMMEDIATE ACTION!

You may think, like I did, that filing for a divorce or having one filed against you is just about the worst thing that could ever happen to you as a married person. I would like to dispel that myth. This is just the inciting incident that sparks of an array of feelings that don't just disappear in a day. I want you to look at divorce as a process; an interruption in your married routine. Everything changes, but as much as it feels like it, it doesn't have to be the end of the world.

I will be honest with you; you may experience shock, you may experience trauma, grief and guilt days, weeks and months after your decree is absolute, but there is a way through this. First and foremost, I would suggest you allow yourself to feel, to experience what you are experiencing and honour how you feel as you go through the process.

Divorce, separation or even a traumatic long-term relationship breakdown has been likened to running the London Marathon. The grief seems so long, and just like the 26 miles it takes to complete the marathon, it just seems to go on and on, never ending. Your stamina, endurance, sanity, resources, faith, patience, confidence, and self-belief is stretched to full capacity. Many a time as you run each lap you may feel broken, unable to go forward, unable to go on, you want to throw in the towel and give up. Yes! Quit. But you can't do that; lives are dependent on you getting through this. Others before you may have buckled under the trauma of divorce, but not you.

You may be asking, "Ok, Zina, thanks for the pep talk, so what do I do to get through this?" The answer is simple: by taking a number of decisive, deliberate, intentional and IMMEDIATE ACTIONS.

IMMEDIATE ACTION 1 – PROMISES

I hereby promise...................

Your **Number 1** immediate action is to set an intention to make unequivocal purpose and passion driven promises to yourself.

Why? Because you are valuable, loved and worthy. Your lovability or worthiness is not dependent upon others, and it is our responsibility to honour and love ourselves even more so when we are feeling unlovable and unworthy. You owe it to yourself.

These are promises which you must never break. Promises to yourself, promises specifically designed to sustain the focus and clarity you need to re-discover the 'me', the 'who you are' after your divorce, separation or relationship breakdown. These are also promises that turn into personal life commitments to yourself. Promises which in turn ignite and inspire you to make a positive difference within your sphere of influence, be the best version of you and propel you towards the accomplishment of your goals and the calling of God upon your life.

I call them the 12 Believe and Live Again Promises.

Thus, as you embark on and navigate through your Believe and Live Again divorce recovery journey, passed the grief and pain towards a brighter tomorrow, I invite and encourage you to make the following 12 promises to yourself each waking day of every week, every month and every year until your divorce recovery is complete.

Exercise 1. Declaring the Believe and Live Again Promises

Believe and Live Again Promises

I hereby declare, decree and promise myself that I will:

1. Take exceptionally good care of my spiritual, emotional, financial, and physical health

2. Stay in the present and not the past so as to reduce worries, stress, anxieties and doubts about my future

3. Acknowledge my fears and limitations

4. Be consistent in my faith and dedicated to my core values and beliefs

5. Act with a spirit of excellence, integrity, optimism, and clarity of purpose

6. Eliminate destructive habits and counter-productive behaviours

7. Consciously seek out and use available tools as well as resources that will help me through my divorce recovery journey so that I emerge renewed, reinvigorated and reinvented with confidence and clarity for the future.

8. Surround myself with trustworthy and supportive people

9. Take consistent and immediate action, even when it makes me feel uncomfortable

10. Make choices and decisions that are aligned with my faith, beliefs and core values

11. Not be hard on myself when self-pity, blame games or negative self-talk threaten to derail during my 'off' periods

12. Actively seek out ways and opportunities to help other people also going through the grief and pain of divorce or relationship breakdown

Why don't you have a go at creating some of your own?

_____

_____

_____

_____

_____

_____

_____

_____

_____

Divorce, just like a marathon, has a way of consuming your life. It becomes who you are. You are now a 'divorced' individual or 'single again' or re-singled. You just don't fit in, but perhaps like me, you didn't want that title and now you are finding it harder than you thought to move on with your life.

Now just the thought of doing simple things, such as going to your local Tesco's supermarket, your down-the-road 24 hours grocery store or even to a nearby Marco Pierre White restaurant where you used to go together, stings you with pain.

If you have children, you will soon discover that in an ideal world divorce is one of those adult events that children don't need to know much about, yet there are so many activities that involve your children where you will find that you miss talking to your spouse about. Even your children inadvertently will find they're missing not having Daddy around so they can boast about him at school, especially after the Summer and Christmas holidays during or Show and Tell if your children are still young or, "my dad bought me a car, or took me shopping or we went to the theatre or we went quad biking on holiday" if they are teenagers, for instance.

You will miss the, "we" sitting at Christmas plays and Sports Days, cheering your children on, taking embarrassing photos and basically being a nuisance together in the audience, when you both talk loudly saying how proud you are of your son or daughter for their recital or sporting prowess or acting ability.

You'll miss the "we" days you could have had with your ex when your children leave secondary education, go off to University, or get married. You'll be consumed with the "what ifs" or "shoulda, coulda, woulda" all over again.

While divorce shouldn't continue to pull on your heart strings forever, it will still break your heart from time to time when you go down the "we" memory lane no matter how bad the marriage may have or not been. The truth is you will have to be intentional and deliberate in learning how to deal with it as much as you possibly can.

8th February 2010 - Morning
Decree Absolute

Dear Journie,

I expected to feel quite sad and kind of surreal but then you know I am overly reflective anyway.

Nothing prepared me for the intense sadness that engulfed me when the Decree Absolute finally came through; my marriage is over. I cried so much which I don't really understand why. I mean he was abusive and the marriage was quite sad a lot of the time. I feel so helpless and hopeless. Why? I guess, just because your spouse was mean to you, it doesn't mean you won't have a broken heart and broken dreams. I mean don't get me wrong, I am relieved that somehow with the help of God I survived the whole miserable saga, but I am definitively not looking forward to the 'divorced' label. I am a Christian woman.

I am feeling a dark gloom envelope like a cloak. I don't need this. I am going out for a walk or something.

Journie, I am really finding it difficult to connect and write in you right now, I am going to have to talk to you later.

Perhaps, this is how you feel right now and you are inwardly screaming, Help! Zina, my Decree Absolute has arrived – how do I deal with the immediate grief and emotional aftermath of the legal end of my marriage? To answer this question, I will share some tips on what not to do, but before that let's go back to my trusted Journie.

8th February 2010
Evening

Guess what? After my brief chat with you this morning, Journie, I went on a long walk and then got onto a tube. When I finally got off at Oxford Circus, I ran into some silly woman on Oxford Street this afternoon. I haven't seen her since 1997. She asked me about my husband and how many kids I had. I told her we were divorced. Unhelpfully, she asked me what I had done. Can you imagine? How insensitive and pompous can one be? She told me how her husband was so wonderful and how wonderful their life together was and asked me why didn't I call her to help me? I am thinking to myself, the last time I saw you was over ten years ago, surely that should tell you, silly goat.

If that wasn't enough, she proceeded to tell me that she always had a strange vibe about my husband, she knew he was up to no good, she could see the signs... and I'm thinking, Lord where are you? Please whisk me away from this insane woman. I then noticed her shoes; they were scuffed and the heels were lopsided. I noticed she was wearing a wig because I could see her scruffy hair peeking out from the nape as she kept on nodding emphatically about how skilled she is at keeping her marriage. She wasn't best pleased when I suddenly burst into laughter. Her shoes and her wig combined set me off. She looked like she was stuck in 1997.

I couldn't really hear what she was saying anymore, thank you, Jesus, because I was laughing so much. I also suddenly noticed that her clothes were ill fitting; her top was miles too low, subjecting my poor eyes to a wrinkly looking ample cleavage, and her coat was too short with two buttons missing from the midriff part of her body while her layers of flab were simultaneously independently going on a rampage through the gap. I mean, Journie, this woman has got to be at least fifteen years older than me. I am sure she has a mirror!

She finally stopped talking at me after what seemed like ten hours but probably was about twenty minutes by telling me, "Zina, don't worry, just look after yourself like I do and if you ever feel like talking, call me." Hell no! Then she said those golden nuggets, those pearls of wisdom... "YOU NEED TO MOVE ON".

There was no 'How'

All the same, I don't think I wanted to listen to another word she had to say. I thanked her profusely, grateful to be "moving on" from her at that point in time, or as my Jamaican friends would say, "galang". Journie, suffice to say, I will never look at Oxford Street the same way after that experience...although to be fair, God did answer my prayers. What started as her making me feel so low, God was able to let me have such a belly laugh.

The Bible says that what the enemy means for bad, God turns it around for good. He definitely did in my case; my mood was sky high, and I went through the rest of the day with a spring in my step, still laughing to myself while on the train. I wouldn't be surprised, I thought smiling to myself, if the woman indignantly thought, "Zina, is so rude, laughing that way, while I was talking to her. No wonder he divorced her".

Not my problem! I can't do much about her thoughts, or her opinions....I haven't mastered mine yet!

I have pondered on this a lot over the years since then, looking back on what transpired between me and that pious and smug woman! I do believe God brought her in at that appointed time for a reason. I guess it was a reflection of how I was feeling at the time. Like a mirror.

Perhaps you are like I was and tend to react a similar way when people glibly say the cliché "you need to move on!" Whenever this was said to me, I used to think angrily to myself *that's easy for you to say*. I never envisaged a life outside being married, so how does one "move on", is there a template? Is there a manual?

If you do find yourself in this position where people are also telling you that you need to move on, chances are that most of the people telling you about the need to move on do not have the foggiest idea how to do it themselves except for giving you empty powerless advice, which in my opinion is a bit like the blind leading the blind. The thing is, as a newly "re-singled" woman, when you stare up ahead of you, you soon realise that you are now at a crossroad in your life. It is completely up to you what path you choose to take.

"The Choices You Make Today Will Determine the Rest of Your Life!"

Experience and hindsight have taught me that "moving on" starts with a choice. As a divorced person, you have all of two choices:

1. **Languish in the Past** or
2. **Flourish into the Future**

You can choose the former by allowing festering anger, bitterness, negative energy, unforgiveness, pain, trauma, and hurt to become your guiding darkness and lock you firmly, hook, line and sinker in the past.

An alternative is, you can make the deliberate and intentional choice to flourish no matter what. This, as well as your faith or guiding power, will begin to align you with your choice and core values to usher in all the light, joy, forgiveness, passion, purpose, clarity, wisdom, fresh opportunities, second chances, and newness of life that moving on attracts.

Throughout my divorce recovery journey, for me it was God Almighty. He was and is my anchor. For you it maybe something different.

Once you have made that choice to move on, the best way to begin to get past a broken heart is to find a way to physically move on with your new found "me" life, yes moving on and singing solo; no longer a duet.

I am not a betting woman, but if I had to hazard a guess, I would say that you probably did not have the time and opportunity to do some of the things you wanted to do while still a "we" in your marriage or long term relationship. Now is the perfect time, the perfect opportunity to go out and do the things you always wanted to do.

Remember, you no longer have to worry about what your ex or anyone else thinks or says about it. You are now in full control of your life; take the reins and gallop, spread your wings and begin to fly, soaring into the sky.

It is a known fact that many a time, individuals go from their parents' home straight into a home of expected wedded bliss and so the chance to be an individual was lost before it had even begun. This has been true throughout time and is still very prevalent in today's world in particular, what with rising prices and temperamental economies. Perhaps this was you, straight from your parent's home into your own home with your husband and then it all came crashing down.

Try and view your divorce as an opportunity to move on and forward by yourself, doing and experiencing the things that you always wanted to do but never had the opportunity to do. Understandably, if you are now a single parent too, this new found freedom must not take priority over the realistic needs of your children.

If you do not have children or other obvious ties, you may want to consider moving away. Most times, just by moving away from the locality will help you to move on and transition a little better and faster than if you stay in the same town or city where you and your spouse once lived.

I am of course mindful of the current economic climate. Studies from across the world, especially in the UK, Canada and the US, show the rising trend in the number of childless ex-spouses that are forced to live under the same roof with each other on account of the cost of living versus the cost of moving and starting over.

Traditionally, when the marriage goes, so goes the house. But with the current economy, more people are finding it difficult not only to sell the family home and divide the proceeds without taking a big loss, but also have the added challenge of being unable to afford to live on their own without that second income the ex-spouse brings in.

There is also research that suggests that divorced couples with children sometimes choose to continue to live together for the sake of their children, but in the main, divorced couples resort to doing this out of financial necessity, reluctantly making the choice to jump from marriage partners to roommates, hoping that the economy and the housing market will turn around and they can sell the home and divide the proceeds sooner rather than later.

This might be the situation you have found yourself in. You cannot afford to move out of the matrimonial home and away from the locality.

Remaining under the same roof as your ex-spouse during and after a divorce can create a host of issues that need to be addressed and considered before reaching any final agreements, including those for property settlement, as well as spousal and child support. Before I talk about some of these issues, let's take a look at the potential advantages or positives; why you and your ex-spouse as well as a host of other divorced couples around the world may decide to continue to live together under the same roof:

Advantages of living together after divorce:

1. **Cost efficiency:** One of the biggest challenges and fears after divorce is in terms of running costs of new separate households instead of one while you were still married. This is often a massive shock to the divorced couple. Consequently, some have found it easier to bury the hatchet to an extent and live as housemates where the bills are shared but not the heart. The outcome is that any savings that occur can be shared equally and perhaps put towards saving to live separately at a future date.

2. **Shared childcare responsibility:** Child care has always been a challenge for parents; this challenge often becomes even more difficult when a couple splits up. The children may find it difficult to cope during the transition, especially if an

ex-spouse moves out. I firmly believe that children especially of school age from say aged three through secondary adjust and cope better under the parenting guidance of both parents under one roof. This, of course, is with the proviso that the home is not a toxic environment.

3. **Grouping resources together:** Recent studies show one of the most common reasons for couples to still live together after divorce is to be able to dip into joint resources in order to pay bills, buy food, make rent or mortgage payments, buy petrol, mechanic, children activities including child care costs. Many couples opt to live together while they put up the family home on sale in order to share the proceeds and then part ways, while other couples stay together until the end of their tenancy or lease so as not to incur a penalty. The key point is that there is an understanding from the start between the ex-spouses or partners that this is a mutually beneficial arrangement with a start and end point. The decision to stay together is objective and dispassionate.

4. **You may become friends.** I have also had some of my clients who have chosen to continue to live together under the same roof state how much better they are as roommates than they were as spouses. I don't know why that is.

Ok, you may have chosen to continue living together but just as a reality check, there must have been a reason the two of you got divorced in the first place. Ask yourself, *how is that going to change, what will be different this time?* In my opinion, it is very unlikely that there is going to a bolt of lightning and suddenly as a result of the "decree absolute" being granted you are both going to change, so much so that the same problems that pulled you apart will suddenly disappear into the abyss. Think about it. Yes, I don' think so! But who am I to think? If you both feel comfortable and don't see it as being impractical to live together now that you are single again, then go for it.

That being said, it is important that you are aware of some potential issues you may encounter that you may need to consider include:

1. How will the family home be divided? What areas including rooms will you and your ex-spouse each have possession over? Will the common areas be divided and if so how?

2. Who will be responsible for paying the household expenses, including groceries, utilities, mortgage, council tax, etc.?

3. Who will be responsible for paying maintenance bills and repairs for the home? Like plumbing, gardening, window cleaning, etc.

4. Do you and your ex-spouse intend to be dating other people? And if yes, will those dates be allowed into the home?

5. A very key issue which I believe will also need to be considered is the issue of sending mixed messages or signals to your children who may still be living in the family home with you. It is important to note that should this be the case, you run the risk of confusing them by you and your ex-spouse continuing to live together.

6. Research suggests that children more readily respond to what they experience rather than what you as their parents may tell them about it. Say for example, if you and your spouse came together one evening after supper and told little Oscar and Jemima that "Mummy and Daddy are divorcing" but they see Mummy and Daddy still giving the impression that they are still married by living together under the same roof in the family home, little Oscar and Jemima may probably forget the whole divorce saga and choose to ignore it any time it is raised, rather believing that nothing has in fact changed in the family dynamics and that the status quo remains the same.

7. In addition, living together after divorce causes even further delays with regard to the children's grieving process causing them to remain in denial longer. This is the same for you too. You may begin to secretly (or not so secretly) have hopes to repair your marriage by attempting to persuade your ex-spouse to get back together again in marriage. My question to you is: *Do you really want to delay the grieving process by raising false hopes of getting back together?*

> *"We are never ever ever getting back together,*
> *We are never ever ever getting back together,*
> *You go talk to your friends, talk to my friends, talk to me*
> *But we are never ever ever ever getting back together"*
> **– Taylor Swift**

8. How will this living arrangement be explained to children, family and/or friends?

9. How long will the living arrangement last? Is there an end-date?

10. What will happen if either you or your ex-spouse wants to leave the home?

11. It goes without saying that living with your ex-spouse after divorce can be extremely problematic when it comes to money. In the past, as a couple you've have agreed on who is responsible for what financially, how joint income is spent, how the joint account is managed and now all bets are off and there are no rules. The issue becomes to what extent do these rules still exist, are new rules required, are you obligated to keep them? My view, without sounding flippant, is if you are in a financially viable position to live separately, then taking a well-deserved holiday is something that you may want to do. Now you have the opportunity – just do it.

I appreciate the huge financial impact that a divorce can cause, however, it is important that you consider these issues very carefully before deciding whether or not to continue to live together under one roof.

Remember, divorce does not have to be a death sentence, instead, if you choose to and are able to change your perspective, it can be the window to a positive new lease of life, a new beginning, with boundless opportunities. And guess what? You may discover that you really enjoy being single.

Studies have also suggested that, after divorce, many adults never re-marry and much of the reason is because they decide they actually like being single.

The fact remains that it is never easy once a marriage ends, believe me I know. Whatever the cause of the split, divorce, separation or even, sadly, death, the breakup of a long-term committed relationship often changes our world and triggers a variety of unsettling and painful emotions.

Painful, because it represents losing, not only a personal connection with someone but shared commitments and dreams. Romantic relationships start on a positive note of hope, goals, and excitement for your future years together.

When I got over the initial denial that my marriage was over, I had no idea where to begin. I had to revaluate and go back to the drawing board of my life, my identity, my relationship with God, my relationship with my children, my living arrangements, my career, child care, my finances, my relationship with my family and my friends, and my dreams. I definitively did not bargain for this, I thought we would live *"happily ever after"*. I guess I thought wrong because the unthinkable had happened and I had to start all over again and I was absolutely terrified. This is why whenever these relationships end, we tend to experience immense disappointment, grief and sometimes, like I did, even shame and guilt. When my marriage first broke down, I mourned it deeply. I mourned for the broken dreams and they were many. Dreams I had built up with my 'wasband', which would now never be. Literally, it was the death of the dream.

I had conjured up dreams about how successful my marriage would be and what the relationship with my 'wasband' would be like. I had clear ideas about sharing a home, romance, sex, having children together, etc. My list was endless. I knew my purpose (or so I thought), had my vision, my 20 year plan, my 10 year plan and my weekly goals, marking them off as I went along.

How so wrong I was!

Looking back at my marriage now, it is so clear that these were not shared dreams or expectations. My dreams were predicated on *forever until death do us part*, not until *divorce do us part*. I did not ever anticipate that there could be another outcome operating under a different set of rules and expectations.

A break up or divorce, as I found, and I imagine that you would discover this immutable fact too, launches us into unchartered territory. The reality you once knew feels like a parallel universe. It seems the same, but it clearly is not. Everything has been uprooted and is floating in the air: our responsibilities and routine, our home, our relationship with extended relatives and friends, as well as our own identities. When your relationship breaks down, it often results in uncertainty and anxiety concerning the future, and these unknowns usually seem worse and more traumatic than the unhappy relationship itself.

I had no idea where to begin. I had to rethink absolutely everything in my life—my home, a job, my identity, my friends, my relationship with my children, and my relationship with God. I had to start all over again.

TEARS ON MY PILLOW!
HOW TO STOP CRYING AFTER DIVORCE

 Tears on My Pillow

Johnny Nash (1975)

I can't take it
I'm so lonely
Gee I need you so
I can't take it
Oh I wonder
Why you had to go

But Baby, Every night I wake up crying
Tears on my pillow
And pain in my heart
You on my mind

I remember all the good times
That we had before
Oh I remember an now my heart
My very soul cries out for more

But baby, all your love for me is dying
Tears on my pillow
Pain in my heart
You on my mind

I'll always remember that day
You promised to love me
You said you'd love me to the very end

And I'll never forget
I'll never forget when you walked away from me
You walked out of my life to my very best friend
Oh

Chapter 2.
DEALING WITH GRIEF

Ok, your Decree Absolute has arrived, your marriage is now legally over and you don't know what to do? The grief and emotional aftermath is crippling.

Don't be surprised if you feel incredibly sad and full of regret. You may even find yourself constantly crying without actually understanding why. On the other hand, you could be happy or just relieved but are really afraid about what people will say about how you feel, so you resort to torturing yourself, thinking if only and what if and how did it get to this?

The long and short is that you are understandably going through a whole wave of various stressful and conflicting emotions. No one teaches you or shows how to deal with this. Your marriage is over whether it was a good one or a bad one, whether you filed the petition for divorce or he did, it is still a loss and adjustments will have to be made.

Studies suggest that a divorce is like a bereavement and, hand on heart, I have to say from personal experience, it is. The Decree Absolute is the final formal decree, it is the final nail in the coffin that has interred your marriage into its grave and sent it into history. Please be encouraged! You are not alone, don't be ashamed, confused or afraid of your feelings as eventually, as the Bible says, "This too shall pass."

Ok, Zina! I hear you say, *so how do I deal with the immediate grief and emotional upheaval now that my marriage is legally over?*

I will unpack this question in **Chapter 3** through sharing some tips of what not to do.

When a marriage or relationship ends, whether you are happy, sad or ambivalent, you may find that your self-esteem is in tatters. Studies suggest that there is a strong likelihood that your perceived acts, failures or omissions, albeit in the past, still gnaw at you and chances are that you are constantly reliving the pain of these experiences. At first, any attempt to focus on your new future by starting over, rebuilding and reinventing your "me" temple may prove to be so difficult.

Rebuilding is all about returning to a state of equilibrium where you are able to rediscover who you once were and reinvent into a better version of "YOU". This is all part of the divorce recovery and healing process.

In simplistic terms, it is about the new choices you make, it is about how you funnel your focus and efforts to what lies ahead in your wonderful new future. In the more complex sense, effective rebuilding is the process of redefining, reframing, reigniting and reinventing YOU, thereby enabling a reconnection with your positive sense of self so that you are able to regain your feminine power and become whole again, spirit, soul and body.

Rebuilding after a relationship breakup like divorce or any other traumatic experience is crucial. If you have made the choice to leave the past behind and stop crying, rebuilding is the only option available to you. Failing that, the very unpalatable alternative would be to remain stagnant in the trauma of your past experience, become buried in the valley of regret and, by so doing, hold yourself to the ideal of reliving and rewriting your past instead of your future.

18th September 2010
Who Am I?

Dear Journie,
Who am I now? Who was I then? Who on earth will I be tomorrow?
Who do I introduce myself as, Mrs? Ms? Miss? Do I change the name on my passport? What about my driving licence?
What do I do with myself now?
I worked so hard to get here, how do I start over again?
Can I ever start over?
Will I ever let myself fall in love again?
How can I stop this pain?

At the very core of this need to rebuild, is the fact that you might be unclear about who you are. For me, in the midst of disappointment over the end of my marriage, I also ended up with a massive identity crisis. You may be going through this too where you feel as if your very identity has been taken away from you. You may even find yourself left with questions for which there are no apparent answers. I know I did, questions like:

- ♥ Who am I now?
- ♥ Who was I then?
- ♥ Who on earth will I be tomorrow?
- ♥ Who do I introduce myself, Mrs? Ms? Miss?
- ♥ Do I change the name on my passport? What about my driving licence?
- ♥ What do I do with myself now?
- ♥ I worked so hard to get here, how am I going to do this all over again?
- ♥ Will I ever be able to start over?
- ♥ Can I ever let myself fall in love again?
- ♥ Will this dull deep excruciating pain ever stop?
- ♥ Can I ever trust anyone enough to fall in love again?
- ♥ When will this engulfing grief ever end?

Experts say that as you attempt to unravel these questions, without you knowing, self-preservation sets in and although you don't realise at the time, in the deepest depth of your subconscious, you begin to hatch the singular plan to regain your positive sense of self. Divorce is wrapped up tightly in deep rooted emotional pain. This pain is so deep, that many feel disassociated. Some of my clients have explained that it is as if they have had a lobotomy without being anaesthetised. Many women, find the divorce experience extremely traumatic *(me included during my own journey)* and often feel so completely disillusioned and disappointed with their new reality that they sadly consider themselves failures.

In order to achieve this goal of re-integration, you have to be willing to include your experience of loss in your self-identity, but without the associated emotional pain. In other words, you have to face head on and incorporate into your identity the loss that you have experienced. This is the ultimate outcome of grieving.

During my own Believe and Live Again divorce recovery journey, I discovered that the process of rebuilding, recovery and reinvention can really only begin after you have successfully grieved the reason or cause behind the disconnection that you feel. Grieving the loss of your marriage paves the way for healing; comfort emerging strength, amazing insight as well as paving the way to the reintroduction to your self- identity.

Another question I often get asked by my divorce recovery coaching clients, and you may be asking too, is, "Zina, how do you know when it is time to undertake the task of rebuilding after a loss?"

There are no hard and fast rules or answers to this, however an effective gauge would be to assess how far along or what stage you are in regarding the grieving process. There are various models that deal with the process and stages of grief. Each stage represents an emotional state. You are ready to rebuild when you have confronted and overcome the challenge associated with each stage.

We all react differently to the grief and loss associated with divorce. However, the pioneering work of Kubler Ross has been extremely helpful and is recognised as the leading authority in identifying the stages of grief.

Kubler Ross's work has been used to identify that there are also common emotional stages of grief that one goes through after a marriage or long term relationship breakdown. These stages draw parallels to the stages of grief experienced at the death of a loved one. At this point, it is important to note that the grieving process is not a linear logical progression through these stages and it is often completely different for each person.

In fact, don't be surprised to find that your emotions and feelings oscillate backwards and forwards through the various stages. This is because, as Dr. Kubler-Ross explained, transitioning through these stages is not a chronological or linear process; in fact in some people the stages overlap and for others they occur in parallel or sometimes get missed altogether. This can be likened to the Reggae song of the 1970's, *"1 Step Forward, 2 Step Backwards"*, from the album *War Ina Babylon*. The learning point here is to know and understand what to expect at each stage as this will help you immensely in finding your way through the grieving process.

The negative feelings associated with grief do not just suddenly disappear, but you will find that some of the stages are easier to navigate than others. The thing to remember is that there is hope in your future and that you will eventually make your way through to healing, recovery and wholeness.

Stages of Grief

"The five stages – denial, anger, bargaining, depression, and acceptance –
are a part of the framework that makes up our learning to live without the one we lost.
They are tools to help us frame and identify what we may be feeling.
But they are not stops on some linear timeline in grief."

– Dr. Elisabeth Kübler-Ross

Here are the 5 grief stages as outlined by the Kubler-Ross model (1969). In 1969, the Swiss-born psychiatrist and author Elisabeth Kübler-Ross wrote the book, *On Death and Dying* reprinted in 1997[2], where she discusses the five stages of grief people go through in order to adjust after the death of a loved one or in the face of their own impending death. This model has also been used to pattern the grief of impending or actual divorce as this also represents loss.

1. Denial – After the initial shock, you will want to cling to a false preferable reality. This can't be happening to me? *"Denial helps us to pace our feelings of grief. There is a grace in denial. It is nature's way of letting in only as much as we can handle." – Dr. Elisabeth Kübler-Ross*

2. Rage and Anger – When denial is no longer a viable option, you will become frustrated and angry. The biggest challenge is how are you going to overcome this burning anger? Especially as you are yet to come to terms with the "whys" and "hows" of your new reality

3. Bargaining – You will begin to 'bargain' with the universe, offering to give up your 'sins' as it were in exchange for having your marriage or relationship back.

4. Depression – Once you recognise that your divorce or breakup is inevitable, you will 'go into hiding', refusing to socialise, feeling sorry for yourself, and throwing pity parties for one. I loved those and had them often – I used to gate crash my own parties, my "pity, under duvet, ice cream eating, never seeing brightness parties for one; star guest: *me, myself and I*". I remember only coming up for air to do the school runs... oh what fun! Not. If you find yourself going through this phase, the biggest challenge you may face is how to overcome the deep sadness and despair. There is nothing prima facie wrong in being in despair or feeling sad when you first experience the trauma of your divorce, however, it is crucial that you will need to get through and over these emotions. The desired result is where you are able to be more dispassionate by simply recognising that the loss of your divorce is a sad event in your life, without the baggage of feeling sad or being depressed. It is not an immediate process but with time, prayers and support it is very achievable.

---

[2] *On Death and Dying* (1969) Kubler-Ross, E (1969), (reprinted 1997)

5. Acceptance – Finally, you have chosen to accept your new reality and have decided it is time to move on and up. This is where you actually begin planning for your new future.

Typical Symptoms of Grief during and after Divorce

To help you identify potential symptoms of grief you may be experiencing or have experienced, I have compiled a list research has shown to be typical symptoms of grief. These typical symptoms are grouped under the headings physical, emotional, cognitive symptoms, spiritual symptoms and social symptoms.

Physical Symptoms of Grief:
- disturbed sleep patterns
- persistent fatigue
- agitation and restlessness
- queasiness and feelings of nausea
- aches, pain and tension in the body
- reduction immunity
- difficulty in stopping activity
- apathy and inactivity
- increased clumsiness

Emotional Symptoms of Grief:
- crying
- sadness
- fear and anxiety
- numbness and/or emptiness
- loneliness
- anger
- helplessness

- irritability
- a sense of observing yourself
- overwhelming guilt
- deflated confidence
- reduced self-esteem
- loss of interest in previously enjoyed activities

Cognitive Symptoms of Grief:

- slowness in processing thoughts
- difficulty in decision-making
- confusion
- daydreams constantly or experience flashbacks of a life that was
- having conversations with divorced ex-spouse or loved one

Spiritual Symptoms of Grief:

- deeper closeness to God
- withdrawal from God
- deep anger at God
- isolation from your church or other religious community
- sensing the divorced your ex-spouses presence

Social Symptoms of Grief:

- prolonged periods of isolation/withdrawal
- self-absorbed, preoccupied with your own emotions, feelings and needs to the exclusion of other people
- relationship stress with your friends, family or colleagues at work
- reduced or complete loss of interest in sex
- displaying impatience with other people you are close with like your children, your parents, or even relatives) who may also be grieving the same loss but possibly in a different grieving style to you

IMMEDIATE ACTION 2 — WHERE ARE YOU?

Exercise 2. **Where Are You In the Grief Process?**

In terms of the stages of grief, have a go at identifying where you are in the grief process and where you want to be or feel.

Stage	How do I feel?	How do I want to feel?
Denial		
Rage and Anger		
Bargaining		
Depression		
Acceptance		

Exercise 3. **Affirmations**

♥ I have every right to feel how I feel

♥ I honour where I feel knowing that feelings are only temporary

♥ I will believe and live again!

Now write five more of your own.

1. _____

2. _____

3. _____

4. _____

5. _____

The Road to Rebuilding is Not Always Linear

The leading authority when it comes to divorce recovery is the book *Rebuilding: When Your Relationship Ends* (Atascadero, CA, Impact Publishers, 1981) written by the late Dr. Bruce Fisher and Dr. Robert Alberti[3]. These doctors developed a proven and effective divorce recovery road map using a nineteen step rebuilding block approach to get your life back together after divorce.

Now the most widely-used approach to divorce recovery, the "rebuilding" model, makes the process healthier and less traumatic for those who are divorcing or divorced—and their children. They carried out a series of group research with those going through divorce and, building upon Kubler-Ross's work, came up with very insightful observations and guidance in how to deal with the stages of grief which occur during and after divorce. *Rebuilding: When Your Relationship Ends* remains the leading authority Divorce Recovery Coaches like myself, counsellors, mediators and psychologists still rely on heavily today.

We cannot expect to go through these stages chronologically, one after another. During my divorce journey, I found there were many times when I really thought I had got over my divorce and then suddenly, like a bolt of lightning, a song or an event or a couple entwined lovingly in each other's arms while going down the escalator in a London Tube station would take me smack right back into an earlier stage of grief. This is a kind of "rehashing" or "recycling". If you find this happens to you, rest assured, it is perfectly normal. If, however, it feels to you that you are stuck in one of these stages for a lingering length of time, I suggest that you consider working with a certified Divorce Recovery Coach like myself or a Relationship Psychologist who is trained to help individuals go through this painful life transition.

The field of Divorce Coaching is wide and collaborates with a team of professionals including pastors, mediators, lawyers, counsellors, psychologists, financial advisors, mortgage brokers and property experts, etc., who would typically work with clients as they transition through the divorce process. 'Recycling' or 'rehashing' is perfectly normal and you will find that it does get easier. The painful episodes will become less frequent and less

---

[3] *Rebuilding: When Your Relationship Ends* (Atascadero, CA, Impact Publishers, 1981) Dr. Bruce Fisher and Dr. Robert Alberti

intense as time goes by. Using the stages of grief, here are some suggestions made in Dr. Fisher's *Rebuilding* book I found helpful and I hope you will too in dealing with the aftermath of divorce.

Stage 1: Denial

When the decision to divorce is made, it is common to at first behave as though nothing has happened. For instance, by not wanting to disrupt the status quo, many carry on life as normal, going about normal routines, burying their heads in the sand and refusing completely to believe the reality of what is happening in their lives. If you are able to draw parallels from this with your life, you are in the denial stage.

During this stage you may also experience a sense of shock or numbness at what has happened, and although you may find yourself keeping up appearances that everything is normal and under control, it is just a facade with you going through the motions and giving the best BAFTA performance of your life. Start keeping a journal. In it, write down both positive and negative feelings. Evidence-based research results demonstrate how important it is to know what you are feeling and what helps you move from one emotion to another. Knowing yourself better is a way to help you in moving away from problem behaviour patterns. It is a well-documented fact that feelings become more powerful if you try to bury them. It doesn't work! Give yourself permission to cry and yell at appropriate times.

Stage 2: Anger

You find that you are absolutely livid and desperately seeking someone to blame for this terrible thing that is happening in your life. Whether you feel it is justifiable anger towards your 'wasband' or ex-spouse or perhaps anger towards your in-laws, parents, friends or even children, it is normal to feel some degree of anger.

I am not an angry or confrontational person by nature. I like being happy and cheerful and consciously seek to avoid unpleasant situations as much as I can, so nothing really prepared me for the gulf of intense anger I felt when my 'wasband' filed for divorce. I mean, he had cheated on me several times and I forgave him. "How dare he!" I found myself thinking, especially when I received the first letter from his solicitors notifying me of his intention to divorce under the "two year rule with consent". I was indignant at the effrontery and also didn't want the divorce label hanging over my head, so I did the only thing I thought I could do at the time. I refused to give my consent to the divorce – i.e. I refused to sign the petition. So now I was not only in denial but was angry too.

At the back of my mind I still believed that suddenly, like I bolt of lightning, my 'wasband' would change his mind, become loving and nice and we would all live happily ever after. Back to reality.

"God hates Divorce". I knew, lived and breathed that scripture from Malachi 2:16 and really wanted so much not to upset God. I think I wanted that more than my marriage itself and I was therefore deeply shocked to discover the degree of anger lingering within me. Rather than take responsibility for my feelings, I blamed my anger on my 'wasband' for breaking up our marriage. I found that discovery really frightening because I truly thought I was ok and never in a million years believed I could feel such a raging emotion.

The scripture *'be angry but sin not'* kept floating in and out of my mind. I sought the help of God by delving deep into His Word – the Bible – to get rid of this anger. I found that because I liked to bury my anger and sweep it under the carpet, dealing with anger was something I had never really learned to do before, so seeking help through God's Word was a valuable process for me.

Anger is a very dangerous emotion and any way you slice it, you and I are responsible for our anger. It is your feeling, it is my feeling, not someone else's.

That being said, projecting the blame for the anger onto someone else is part of the recovery and rebuilding process but eventually, as I found out and you will too, you must take full responsibility for your own anger.

In the Fisher Divorce Adjustment Scale, there is a powerful anger statement:

"I blame my former lover-partner
for ending our love relationship."

Yeah, I know, I guess you are not that unique! That is exactly how I felt too. Maybe this is where you are at now.

Using the Fisher Divorce Adjustment Scale, deeper research into this indicates that those who agree with this statement: **"I blame my former lover partner for ending our love relationship"**, may have not yet dealt with their anger sufficiently. However, those who disagree have come to the realisation that through the rebuilding and recovery process they have made significant progress in their anger and are able to see that failure, blame and responsibility are bi-directional, that is, that both parties are responsible.

It is a well-documented and proven fact that people who are unable to move past the anger become bitter. This can be the most difficult stage to really completely shift, and it can take a few years.

Apart from anchoring myself deeper in God, to get through this stage, I found people who I could laugh and cry with. Two couples, T and B and M and A, parents of two primary school friends of my oldest daughter from when they were all in Reception class together. Our daughters also attended weekly swimming lessons together, so through the whole parent-in-primary-school experience, the school plays, school governorship, school fetes, sports day, parents' evening, and Saturday swimming lessons, the two mothers in particular and I became firm friends. Our daughters, who have since grown up as they do, (yeah!) with the lashes, long hair extension and impeccable makeup, are now all in university, but we, the mums, remain best friends till this day, many years later, celebrating our victories and helping each other as we get through a host of everyday life challenges.

It is often said that I have a cheerful, friendly, funny, warm and chatty disposition. I guess only others can be the true judge of that. What I do know is that I have the tendency to put a positive and humorous spin on most things and my divorce was no different. I even joked (when I wasn't crying that is) about how awful the whole experience was, often making wise cracks or doing impromptu stand-up routines about some of the unpleasant things that were happening to me. It was wonderful to be able to share that humour with both couples without feeling awkward or being made to feel like a "sorry case".

The Bible says in Proverbs 17:22 NLT:

**"A cheerful heart is good medicine, but
a broken spirit saps a person's strength".**

I firmly believe that humour can help you stand outside your situation, get a perspective, and not get stuck in a victim mentality. Please don't get me wrong, I will be the first to admit that I did have pity parties, really regular at first, duvet clad events 'for one' with my massive Häagen Dazs ice cream tub, watching reruns of *Sleepless in Seattle*, but thankfully they became quite short lived very quickly. If you are reading this and love holding pity parties too, don't beat yourself up about it, but do make sure you are able to draw or anchor yourself in God if you are a person of faith as well as having a strong network of trusted friends and family who you know will happily be relentless in gate-crashing your 'parties for one' to set you free from yourself when you need it most.

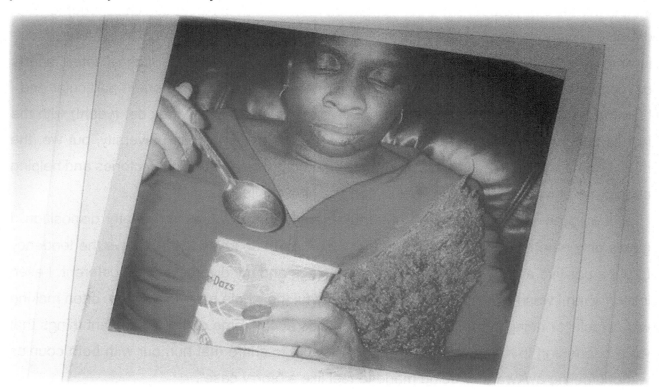

I am exceptionally blessed to have a wonderful support network of close friends and family on almost every continent in our world who said things like "what's happened to you is so awful, it is hilarious!"

Those friends refused to let me drown and kept my spirits up so that I didn't lose my signature big smile and my uproarious sense of humour even during my darkest moments. This group of amazing people helped me focus on what I was going to do next at every given time, rather than allowing me to wallow for too long in my famous pity 'parties for one' and be held back in a miserable past.

Now, I am not suggesting you should be the class clown or the court jester. I am not even suggesting that you force yourself to laugh at what you are going through if you are not that way inclined. What I am saying is that it is important to have a trusted support network of friends and family who are your personal cheerleaders. People who are able to laugh and cry with you but also not allow you to linger too long in the dark.

Today, long after my divorce recovery, I still laugh with my friends at some of the silly things I did and said in the run up to my divorce and while going through it. A good example is me perpetually searching for my children's passports. I would typically hide them away somewhere safe, so safe that I would never remember where. Getting the girls and myself prepared for family holidays abroad were an absolute nightmare. I would buy the flight tickets, pay for the hotel and then spend over two weeks ransacking my home from top to bottom, trying to find these passports. Somehow, through some divine intervention, I would find the passports in the nick of time, maybe under the carpet or behind the boiler or some other obscure place and rush out of the house, which looked like a bomb site, straight to the airport.

The thing was that my "wasband" still had the keys to the family home and at the time I was absolutely terrified that he would come in while I was away at work and take away our daughters' passports in order to kidnap them at a later date and send them to Africa.

If you are reading this and you have identified that you are in the anger stage of grief, can I strongly suggest you find creative ways unique to you to express that anger? If you are at a loss as to what ways to use, try punching pillows, competitive sports, screaming your head off while alone in front of your bathroom mirror or whilst driving alone in the car.

Personally, I am a torrential crier. The floods flow. You may want to try that too: crying, laughing till you cry or crying until you laugh at yourself; really let yourself go, let the flood gates of tears fall. I can assure you that this is very cathartic. You will find it to be a very powerful way of reducing stress and anger. You might not think so, but take it from me, it is actually very beneficial and productive to be angry as you go through divorce.

What? Zina, are you for real? Yes, I am because anger allows us to begin to let go and become emotionally distant from our exes. Studies have shown that people who are unable to express anger during divorce or a relationship breakdown take much longer to let go and get over the trauma. They often find themselves going through long bouts of depression and stay stuck in the past, unable to stop the strong feelings they have for their ex.

My advice, is to let your anger be released and expressed as freely as possible, but in appropriate ways that do not harm you or put others at risk.

A wonderful and effective way to express anger I found particularly useful is to call a close friend or family member and say, "Petra, I need to talk about this anger that I am feeling towards my ex, it is driving me crazy. I know I may not always make sense and I know that I may become very emotional. And I know that some of the things I say might not be what I am really feeling all the time. But right now, I am feeling really angry and I need you to hold the space for me and listen to me talk about my anger." This person is a life line support friend or relative, someone you trust inherently to help you through these times. Trust me; it is one of the best tools for dealing with anger.

Another effective way is to write a letter expressing all the things you would like to say to your ex. Write it in big letters, perhaps in red marker or crayon, write it with lots of anger. Please do not post it but burn it up. This effectively becomes symbolic of expressing and then burning up your anger or destroying it completely.

My personal favourite, from which many of my coaching clients have been able to achieve major shifts and transformation, is the "empty chair", an effective Gestalt therapy technique. In this technique, a chair is brought out and you imagine you're ex sitting on the hot seat. You say everything you have ever wanted to say to him. If you want to take it even further you can switch positions and sit in the chair to say everything you wish your ex would say to you in return. It might seem counter intuitive but this technique is particularly effective. At the end of the day, just seek any form of help that is productive and works for you. The golden rule is to allow yourself to be vulnerable as you release your anger.

However, if your feelings seem to be getting out of control or become directed against the wrong people, your children in particular, then you should seek professional help fast! During this stage, you may also have to deal with the anger of others. For instance, your children, if you have them, may be harbouring these feelings of anger, blaming you for the family break-up, or your ex-spouse may feel angry at you if you were the person who initiated the divorce.

As Dr Fisher suggests, make an anger list. It's easy to fantasise and idealise that your former partner and the marriage were wonderful and you feel they are unbearable to lose. An anger list will help you be more realistic and figure out what your anger triggers are.

Three phases of dealing with anger described in *Rebuilding* are:

1. Accepting that it's okay to feel angry

2. Learning how to express anger constructively

3. Forgiveness

From working with hundreds of women, I can say that Forgiveness is the most difficult. But the ability to Forgive is not for your ex but for YOU. See it as an enormous gift that you give to yourself, the gift of being empowered and released from that huge weight of anger weighing you down and stifling your emotional growth. Forgiveness not only for your ex but also to yourself for any part you may have played in your marriage or relationship breakdown.

In Rebuilding: When Your Relationship Ends, Dr. Bruce Fisher and Dr. Robert Alberti strongly suggest that anger not only needs to be vented but also needs to have a channel of release. Channels of venting and release are different for each person, if you are wondering what might work for you, here are some of my tried and tested methods.

Humour has always been my default stance, it might not be yours if your temperament is more of a sanguine nature, but you never know. Some of the best comedians around the world have come from having experienced or being close to someone who has been affected by some form of trauma.

Another excellent release channel is going to the gym or even just going for early morning jogs. Studies show that when you exercise your body emits chemicals known as endorphins which go a long way to relieve stress, depression and alleviate anger by causing you to go into a happier state.

I am not an angry or confrontational person by nature. I like being happy and cheerful seeking to avoid unpleasant situations as much as I can, so nothing really prepared me for the gulf of intense anger I felt when my ex-husband filed for divorce.

You may feel the same but my advice to you is to honour how you feel and make a pledge to know that you can and you will move into a better sphere

Exercise 4. **The Anger List**

Sometimes we may feel so angry and bottle it in. This is called suppressed rage and can be extremely harmful for us. So I suggest, go on, make that piñata and bash it as hard as you can with a stick, scream at the top of that hill and let it all out and if that is a bit dramatic for you, try my *Anger List* exercise.

The objective of this exercise is to identify your anger triggers.

♥ Do you get really angry when your ex calls the children?

♥ Does the sound of his voice make your blood curdle?

♥ Does a particular perfume remind you of his affairs because of the same one you found hidden in his socks drawer that you thought was your Christmas present, only to find an unceremonious envelope under the Christmas tree with a £50 M&S gift voucher?

♥ Perhaps a song played on the radio reminds you of your first dance and then with that memory you get so incredibly angry?

Whatever your anger triggers are, make a list.

Goal: To better understand your automatic reactions or triggers which contribute to your anger.

Instructions: Reflect upon your memories, thoughts, characteristics or experiences relating to your ex that evoke significant angry feelings within you.

List: The Anger triggers:

1. Hearing the voice of your ex on the telephone

2. The smell of a particular perfume

3. Your ex not turning up to pick up the children on the agreed day

4. His letters arrive yet again because they have not been redirected to his new address

These are only examples; have a go at writing down some of your own:

_____

_____

_____

_____

_____

_____

_____

_____

_____

_____

_____

Stage 3: Bargaining

This is the stage where you become almost desperate, you feel ready to do anything so things will go back to the way they were. "I remember saying to God, "Just give me my life back" even though, clearly, my marriage had been over for a long time. It is normal to try to avoid the inevitability of the end of a marriage by bargaining, either with your ex-spouse or with yourself. You may find yourself promising to change certain parts of your behaviour if only you can have another chance. I remember suddenly seeing my abusive marriage as a sacrificial cross that I should bear. I begged God that if He saved my marriage, I would be the best wife ever whether my husband treated me well or not. I was prepared to go through it because I wanted to keep up the appearances of remaining married and not have the stigma of being divorced. It sounds absolutely ridiculous now, but looking back, it was my way of trying to stop the pain I was feeling, which for some reason became distorted in my mind's eye and so much worse than the sum total of the years I had spent in my traumatic and abusive marriage.

I remember pursuing my ex-husband, wanting him back at all costs to me and to the detriment of my self-esteem. If this is you, please don't beat yourself up for trying to bargain. This stage happens because you're trying to stop the pain you are feeling; it can also be an indication of you attempting to take back some control over the situation. Please, please please try your best to see this for what it is; it is not some indication or green light to get back together, it is just another stage in the process.

Stage 4: Letting Go

This stage can be very difficult, because it may come with a recurrence of depression and even suicidal thoughts. I remember not being able to get out of bed on many occasions during this stage. I also recall the sadness I felt; that debilitating sadness became my constant companion. This is the one stage most divorcing or divorced people should expect will hit them at some point. This helps you become better prepared for the inevitable.

It is also the stage when you can begin to focus on finding new meaning in your life and making new choices. It may be a good time to consider receiving counselling or joining a divorce recovery coaching group like Believe and Live Again or another kind of support group to work and support you through letting go. The support of family and friends is also invaluable to you during this stage.

Stage 5: Acceptance

You finally come to a place of acceptance as if you are saying to yourself, "Ok, I can deal with this new era. It is what it is and I can make the best of my new life without him." Suddenly, you feel able to exhale. You come to a reborn fresh outlook and understanding that the sum total of your life is not determined by your marital or relationship status. You come to a time and space in your life where you are able to see things from a new perspective and see opportunities and possibilities.

At this stage, many women find they are full of new energy to try new things such as going on an adventure they would never have dreamt of. Perhaps you may consider going on a cruise, travelling the world, parachuting, power gliding, backpacking expeditions in the Australian Outback, teaching English in the remotest regions in the Amazon. You may join a church or become a volunteer with a wonderful charity, try new foods around the globe, go wine tasting, visit art galleries, learn to play a new instrument or just shop till you drop. ☺ The list is endless.

18th September 2011
I can't sleep

Dear Journie,

Sometimes I get so overwhelmed. I lie awake at night because I just can't sleep, yet I am so tired and so restless. I have aches and pains all over. I feel so helpless and always I am engulfed in a sea of mental confusion with intermittent flashbacks. Will I ever get over my hurt so I can be a normal mummy again to the girls?

I am also angry because he told me he would never hurt our family like his dad did to him, his sibling and his mother; but now it's as if history has come full circle and that was indeed what he has done.

I only discovered the other day when we exchanged Form E that he has become engaged, moved into a new home with another woman, they have one son, and she is pregnant with the second child. I mean, he is well within his right to do this and I don't mind that he has moved on, but it seems to me to be at the expense of our daughters. He habitually fails to show up when he has arranged an outing with them and is not really as involved as I feel he should be in bringing them up - especially emotionally.

Now I am the sole breadwinner, support, career, cab driver and parent; this is not what I signed up for. I never wanted to do this alone. I am so so so tired. I am drowning. I am always in floods of tears but yet I have to keep smiling... keep my happy face on with my eyes glazed as if in a trance. All this effort..just to get through the day. I wear this mask whether at home, at church or at work and yet everyone thinks I am ok! I have just got to keep it together for the girls. It really isn't their fault. I am the parent and I have to keep going to alleviate the gravity of emotional pain and stress they are going through for something they had nothing to do with. They don't even understand why any of this has taken place. And because I am the life and soul of any gathering, I feel so completely alone. I gave him my whole heart. I trusted him; I loved him to the moon and back. How did I get it so wrong?

Journie, I wish you could help more! I don't know where else to go. Sure my friends offer, but they just don't know what I'm really going through. I am glad at least I can pour out my heart into you.

Looking back, I didn't realise the pain was so deep. If this is you right now, I get that. Although your story and your journey may be different from my own experience, I can appreciate that devastating feeling of having trusted your spouse or partner (if you lived together but were not legally married before the break up) wholeheartedly, only to be overwhelmingly disillusioned by the discovery that your trust was grossly misplaced. It's all about our relationship expectations which are now unenforceable.

If you're reading this and are anything like me, perhaps you held core beliefs and values about what you thought life should look like and how people should be. You believe in trust, honesty and integrity. You believe, just like I did, that marriages should be forever, "till death do us part". You believe that a father should be there for his children. You believe that your ex should step up to the plate, offer both financial and emotional support and accept responsibility. These are all good beliefs.

Our beliefs lead us to expect a certain level of behaviour from others as well as expectations about life. However, here's the problem! People, as you have discovered, do not always live up to our own expectations and do not hold the same beliefs. An unenforceable expectation is one that we cannot enforce, we cannot control. That is what you have right now and it is unenforceable. You may be grieving the breakdown of your marriage, oscillating to and fro between and through the various stages of grief, however, here's the thing; what we cannot control we must accept and let go. By not doing this, we, sadly, run the risk of allowing the grief to eat us up from the inside out. This is probably one of the most important lessons I have learnt in my life. I want to gift this same valuable lesson to you now so that your own divorce recovery journey, transition and healing is much swifter, smoother and deeper than mine ever was.

Why go through this needless pain if someone else has already gone through it ahead of you? Like I soon discovered and so will you too, try as you might, you cannot control his actions or the way he thinks. For your own sanity and emotional wellbeing, it is best you learn to let that all go and accept 'what is' versus what you think 'should be'.

What is…that's the new reality. In this new reality, recognise the things you can control and the things you cannot. What really helped me was the age old serenity prayer. It might help you too:

"God grant me the serenity to accept the things I cannot change;
the courage to change the things I can;
and the wisdom to know the difference."

– Reinhold Niebuhr

Accepting 'what is' is a wonderful way to learn how to inculcate the spirit of serenity during the often devastating experience called divorce. It is a valuable way of identifying patterns of behaviour or personality that need to change.

Exercise 5. Divorce Recovery Change List

Have a go at developing a two column table that will house traits you can change and those you cannot. Being intentional in this way helps you not to spend unnecessary effort, emotions and energy on things that you cannot change and have no business trying to change. For instance your divorce or other people's opinions about you. The rule of thumb is to expend your energy on activities that will bring God glory and help you move forward.

Change	Cannot Change

That new reality is all about you now. It is about taking care of yourself and taking responsibility for the new you. This includes doing those things that will alleviate the effects of all the grief, the tears and the stress associated with your divorce or you will break down.

Take for instance: Exercise! It is well proven that this is the number one antidote to stress. Look into joining a gym class like Boxercise, Step, Aerobics, Spinning, Circuit, Leg, Bums and Tums, Aqua Aerobics, etc.; the list is endless. Take a trip to your local gym for details of the available group classes and how to join. How about dance classes like Salsa, Zumba, or Street? These classes will definitely burn down the stress levels and extra pounds you may have lurking under your oversized hoodie or sweats.

The important thing is to schedule in time for yourself. Eat well and get plenty of sleep. If you are a parent, why don't you provide yourself with generous lashings of the same kind of nurturing and compassion that you give your kids? After all, you deserve it too.

In addition to this, please don't try to do this alone; get support! Get help! A good place to start is **meetup.com**. Search for a divorce support group in your area. As a Born Again Christian, I strongly subscribe to also seeking support from counsellors in your local assembly, if they are sympathetic, trained and supportive of members who may be going through a divorce experience. Go to your pastor or clergyman for prayers if that works for you; whatever you do, talk to a professional.

Sadness is often seen as a sign of weakness. An anomaly. What compounds matters is the fact that we often try to rebuild our lives after the trauma of divorce without allowing ourselves the space and time to grieve instead, we give the appearance of "we are fine"; "everything is ok"; that it is "business as usual."

It is not just okay to grieve; it is a sign of healthy functioning.

To me grieving is like a cleansing.
It tells your inner self that it is time to begin
the process of working on the new.

Equally important in undertaking the task of rebuilding and recovery is the understanding you have of your life stage. This concept is premised on a developmental approach to human behaviour and functioning. In this context, your response to a loss is understood as partly influenced by your life stage.

Finding yourself in a position where you are able to understand what stage you are in during or after divorce is of enormous benefit. It helps in being appreciative of the elements of your life that have been most adversely affected by the divorce trauma and associated loss. As a result, you will often find in the quest to understand your feelings of grief that you will also be empowered to redirect and intensify efforts to rebuild your life.

Ngozi's Story – Life Stages Case Study

To better illustrate the importance of life stages in rebuilding and divorce recovery, let's consider for a moment a life stage case study concerning Ngozi – a fifty five year old woman who experienced divorce from her husband Ola after 28 years of marriage.

Ngozi was absolutely devastated; she felt as if her world had just fallen apart. Experts say that a midlife divorce is harder than at any other time. This was certainly the case for Ngozi. She had spent her life raising the kids, running the home and supporting her husband with erudite precision and selfless dedication. She had readily lost herself and career in her marriage; her life, purpose and aspirations were subsumed into Ola, her husband's vision.

Her kids had now grown up, the last one – a daughter – was away in university studying medicine; another one, her middle child, a son, had left home right after university and joined the British Army, while the oldest, another daughter, married to a pastor, was away in the mission field in Papua New Guinea. Ngozi had never seen her grandchildren, her menopause was kicking in and her aged Nigerian parents now living in their home needed around the clock care.

With Ola gone, deep within the tentacles of a 28 year old "Rhianna" look alike sales and marketing executive, Ngozi felt her life was empty, devoid of purpose and meaning. She often experienced moments throughout her day where she felt totally lost, overwhelmed and desperate. Anger, shock, sadness, denial and pain seemed to take over her life. Her feeling of grief was all engulfing; she was bewildered. How could divorce happen to us? She was blindsided by her husband, she never saw it coming; she had committed most of her life to her marriage, and now betrayed at aged 55, she had nothing.

Her 'wasband' Ola was moving on in his new life with ease. *How could he?* she shouted in anguish to no one in particular. Just when Ngozi was looking forward to taking life a bit easier and starting the twilight stage of their marriage together, especially now that the children had grown up and more or less fled the nest, she was faced with anger, loneliness and fear. She was completely at a loss of how to navigate her future. Can there really be a good and positive life for her ahead?

It's harder than divorce at other times (the kids getting older, then there is menopause looming, parents needing more care). It's unbelievably painful, like a personal tornado, and no one seems to really get what you're going through.

Although, I was nowhere near 50 at the time of my own divorce years ago, I am there now and appreciate how one might feel that there is no way to get through this personal tornado to create a life that's awesome and most times even better than before.

At *Believe and Live Again Post Divorce Lifestyle Coaching*, we provide tailor made strategies for every professional woman, female entrepreneur or woman of faith from ages 25 – 75 to navigate this trip with fewer tears and more quickly than if you struggle through on your own. Age is just a number and for this reason we give you tools to deal with the overwhelming emotions… despair, loneliness, fear, anger, hopelessness… and we help you stop obsessing about him and start concentrating on building your own best life.

From my own personal experience, I understand that a one-sized post-divorce recovery strategy does not fit all. In the Ngozi case study, this was a midlife situation where Ngozi's focus in rebuilding would most likely be different than the focus of a 25 year old woman experiencing a divorce after three years of marriage.

By working with Ngozi to know and understand the significance of the various aspects of her life that have been impacted by her experience of divorce, Ngozi as a 55 year old woman becomes empowered, becoming more able to understand why she feels the way she does and on what aspects of her life she needs to concentrate her rebuilding efforts. In this case study, although both women may be going through a similar devastation and emotional pain, their grief is likely to be different based on the meaning off loss and the life stage they are in. The women in this case study may be experiencing a similar kind of loss. They may both feel pain but they might actually be grieving over totally different things as determined by the meaning of the loss they are experiencing. This may be based on the difference in their life stage.

The learning point here is to seek professional help as soon as possible if you find you are experiencing trouble grieving the loss and/or transitioning through the different stages of grief. Please seek professional help too if either you or your friends/family have expressed concerns about the sheer intensity of your feelings of loss or the length of time you have spent grieving.

A very crucial part of the jigsaw in the grieving process and rebuilding your life after divorce is to process the unresolved residues of regret, guilt, shame, and blame you may be feeling or projecting onto your ex-spouse. Without chiselling away at these residues and getting through them, it is difficult to rebuild. If you haven't and are trying to rebuild, it is on shaky ground, where the slightest incidence of emotional upheaval runs the risk of causing significant damage.

Again, seek professional help if you find yourself unable to work through these feelings on your own.

In the final analysis, rebuilding and the grieving process are interrelated; you cannot rebuild without first grieving.

Grieving is healthy and the first key to recovery, emotional healing and reinvention after divorce. The tears on your pillow and the pain in your heart will eventually stop, but only when grieving cycle is complete.

It is important to stress here that at any time, either during your grieving process or when rebuilding so that you can Believe and Live again, you may need to seek professional help in order to explore the importance of your stage of life, work through potential feelings of guilt, shame, self-blame and regret, or as a source of support.

At Believe and Live Again, apart from 1 to 1's, we also offer group coaching which has proved extremely effective and popular in overcoming the emotional pain of any kind of loss. For many, however, individual coaching is the best means of receiving optimal help.

Help, I have just been served with papers, what do I do?

Up until now, I have been talking about what to do after divorce and you might be reading this thinking, *Zina, what about me? I need help too, I have just been served with divorce papers, what do I do?* So here, we will be going back in time to the period where you knew, realised or uncovered and admitted to yourself that divorce was on the cards. Let's go to the very beginning.

 Doe a Deer

From the Film *The Sound Of Music*

Let's start at the very beginning
A very good place to start
When you read you begin with A-B-C
When you sing you begin with do-re-mi
Do-re-mi, do-re-mi
The first three notes just happen to be
Do-re-mi, do-re-mi
(Maria)
Do-re-mi-fa-so-la-ti
(spoken)
Let's see if I can make it easy
Chorus
Doe, a deer, a female deer
Ray, a drop of golden sun
Me, a name I call myself
Far, a long, long way to run
Sew, a needle pulling thread
La, a note to follow Sew
Tea, a drink with jam and bread
That will bring us back to Do (oh-oh-oh)

If you were the person who initiated the divorce (petitioner), your solicitor would normally have commenced the process by sending an initial letter to the respondent (your wasband) to tell him of your plans to commence divorce action. This letter also recommends that your husband or wife gets independent legal advice ASAP if they have not done so already.

> *March 18 2006*
> *Name of Solicitor*
> *Street Address*
> *London*
> *NW5*
>
> *Dear Madam,*
> **Notice of intention to commence divorce proceedings.**
> *Your husband, Dr P Person, has instructed us to notify you of his intention to commence divorce proceedings against you. We understand that your marriage has broken down irretrievably as you have both lived apart from each other continuously for an upwards of three years.*
> *We will send you a copy of the petition we intent to file in court on our client's, your husband's behalf.*
> *We therefore strongly urge you, if you have not already done so, to contact your solicitor to act on your behalf and respond within 7 days of receiving this letter.*

This is an excerpt of the letter I received. When it first arrived I went hysterical, I withdrew into myself with sadness, then I was confused, I cried and cried and cried, then the anger came. Imagine the effrontery of my 'wasband', I thought? I zeroed in on the lies. We had not lived apart continuously for three years and who gave him the audacity to file against me? And guess what? In denial, I refused to respond or even acknowledge the letter, hoping the state of affairs would go away.

If you are reading this and you are not divorced but you are either applying for a divorce or your spouse is, the process is typically initiated with an "Initial Letter to the Respondent". You may have received or given instructions for one to go out similar to the one I got years ago. Here is a brief overview of what to expect after that.

The Divorce Process (UK, 2016)[4]

The legal formality of getting a divorce is a relatively straightforward process. What is generally much less straightforward is sorting out the practical issues associated with a divorce, such as where each person will live, who gets what and arrangements for any children. Before agreeing to matters with your husband or wife, it is wise to take advice from a solicitor about your rights and the options available to you.

---

[4] Cited from *http://www.lawsociety.org.uk/for-the-public/common-legal-issues/getting-a-divorce/*

The Legal Terms Used in Divorce[5]

In court and in legal documents, the person applying for the divorce is known as 'the petitioner', and the person they are divorcing is 'the respondent'.

Initial Letter to the Respondent

If you are applying for the divorce, your solicitor will usually start the process by writing a letter to your husband or wife to tell them that you are planning to start divorce action, similar to the one I received and mentioned earlier. This letter will also recommend that your husband or wife gets independent legal advice if they have not done so already.

Divorce Petition[6]

Your solicitor will then send the divorce petition to the court. The petition sets out whether you will be asking your husband or wife to pay for the costs of the divorce or to provide some other sort of financial support for you or your children. The court will send a copy of the petition to your husband or wife for their solicitor to reply. Once your husband or wife or their solicitor has replied to the petition, you will need to confirm your intention to go ahead with the divorce application by making a sworn statement or 'affidavit'. Your application is then lodged with the court. If your husband or wife does not reply or cannot be found, your solicitor will tell you the methods for overcoming this.

---

[5] Cited from *http://www.lawsociety.org.uk/for-the-public/common-legal-issues/getting-a-divorce/*
[6] Cited from *http://www.lawsociety.org.uk/for-the-public/common-legal-issues/getting-a-divorce/*

IMMEDIATE ACTION 3 –
TAKE TIME OUT TO DISCOVER YOUR INNER COPING MECHANISM

During the sadness and stress of my own divorce, although I did not know it at the time, an internal survival mechanism had set in which caused me to seize the opportunity to gain from the experience and grow into the wiser, stronger, Believe and Live Again woman I am today. Through my experience, I was able to uncover the real me inside, find my authentic self, the true essence of who I am and what I have been brought into this earth to do. I never thought I would ever say this but it has been the most amazing, phenomenal journey of my life; each day, each month, each year I keep discovering parts of me I never even knew existed, talents, new skills, new visions, drive, passions, new purpose and the creation of new realities... and guess what? I am still on this amazing journey of self-discovery and self-actualisation and it is so fun and full of intrigue. I would be lying if I said this is what I set out to do, however rather than allow yourself to go through what I did, you can start here, right now and be intentional about your recovery – regain control of your life.

Before we begin, it is imperative that you understand the importance of having a post-divorce support network that you can turn to and confide in when the stress and trauma of the relationship breakdown takes its toll. You might recall that I talked about getting support and help briefly under **Immediate Action 2**. I will go into a bit more detail in Chapter 3.

Everything written in this book will guide you along your recovery journey, but there are two vital behaviours that I believe you need to start cultivating immediately to ensure this process is as painless as it can be.

Firstly: Refuse to allow yourself to be isolated – Get support ASAP!

Secondly: Understand the need for and start cultivating new friendships.

Chapter 3.
GUILT AND ISOLATION!

Support from other people is crucial to healing following a break up or divorce. I often felt like just being on my own after my divorce, but cutting myself off from friends and family ultimately just made this period harder. As the saying goes: "No man (or woman) is an Island" so do not attempt to cope with this by yourself. You might find that many of the friends you had together as a couple will have taken sides, so your network of friends will reduce anyway; isolating yourself further will do you no good whatsoever.

For those of you reading this who are Christians, you will know that one of the chief ploys of the devil is to cause you to be isolated through whatever means possible. A good case in point is the story of Prophet Elijah in 1 Kings 19 who, despite his great faith, fell into depression, going from the mountain top to the valley.

At the mountain top, Elijah had experienced one astonishing miracle after another. God had sent ravens to feed him. Through Elijah, a widow and her son were miraculously provided for during drought and famine. Elijah even raised the widow's son from the dead! Then Elijah called down fire from heaven while confronting a group of antagonistic idol-worshippers. As a result, there was a sweeping revival in the nation.

The last thing we would expect is for Elijah to fall into depression, but he did. He was tired and isolated, he spiralled downward; even suicidal thoughts were part of his dark episode.

"He prayed that he might die, and said, 'It is enough! Now, Lord, take my life, for I am no better than my fathers!'" (1 Kings 19:4).

Elijah's situation reveals several problems that can bring us down.

Mental health professionals also agree that it is through isolation that your mind gets attacked with thoughts like *"I am not good enough"*, *"everyone hates me"*, *"it was all my fault" my life is over"* *"I will never find anyone to love me again"* *"I can never forgive him, he/she ruined my life"* *"I can never trust anyone with my heart again"*, and so on.

I admit, I once had some of these thoughts too. One thing I did (which is a very good coping mechanism) was to get in touch with trusted family and friends, especially those who had experienced painful divorces or break ups themselves. They understood to a certain extent what I was going through because they had gone through it too. I found that they were empathetic, plus they were able to assure me that healing and new relationships were something that I could look forward to in the future.

In addition to guilt and isolation you may also feel intense shame. In spite of how you may be feeling now, if you get anything from this chapter, let it be that your divorce or relationship breakdown is nothing to be ashamed of.

Outsiders may judge you, especially if you are a woman of faith. You may find that many of your friends and family in your faith community, for instance Christianity, are unsupportive and unforgiving, often inadvertently making you feel like a sinner and dirty failure. It could even be worse if your friends and family thought that from the 'outside' your relationship looked perfect. They might accuse you of ending the relationship unfairly or of having ulterior motives like cheating. Others may try to make you feel ashamed simply because they don't approve of divorce. In Christendom, the Bible scripture in Malachi 2:16, "God Hates Divorce", quickly comes to the fore. It could be that they are friends with your ex-spouse. Some might even say you're ruining the lives of your children. You have sinned against God and are therefore unworthy.

My advice? Ignore them all!

The feeling of shame can go deeper than guilt. This is because shame is not based on having done something wrong so much as a soul ache of being wrong at the core; and if you let it, feeling ashamed because of your divorce can be so debilitating, isolating and more piercing than condemnation especially as a woman of faith.

I understand first-hand the degree of shame which could engulf you. However, whatever your belief systems are, shame can have such far reaching effects on your life.

Here is a short, but definitely not comprehensive, list.

1.   As a Christian, shame puts you in bondage of self-perception. Although you really deeply want to believe all of the wonderful things that the Bible says about you, you find that you just can't.

2.   Shame has the ability to handcuff you to your past. You want to hope for better things in the future, but you can't seem to overcome your past.

3.   Shame won't let you receive love and will definitely not give it. You become unable to receive or accept authentic compliments and you tend to destroy otherwise healthy relationships.

4.   Being ashamed steals your joy. "Where is this abundant life the Bible promises?"

5.   Experiencing shame because of your divorce could potentially make you settle for less than you deserve. God wants to lead you into wonderful relationships and abundant blessings, but you could find yourself making poor decisions and living in regret.

6.   Feeling ashamed of yourself can result in you becoming withdrawn and depressed.

Studies suggest that shame regarding a divorce can be both internal and external. It can come from the misguided opinion of others or it can come from within yourself, your own guilty conscience or bad feelings.

The brutal truth is that some relationships work out and some just don't. You just have to accept that, whether the divorce was your choice or not.

Think of it almost as a second chance, a fresh reinvented start for you to be who you really deserve to be.

To get through this difficult period in your life you need to face the truth. Some people will be there for you and some won't. Accept that some of the people you considered 'friends' when you were with your ex will choose to support him or her and not you. Just accept it and move on with the friends you can count on because it is crucial that we spend time with the people who add to, support, value and energise us. So please choose wisely.

When I was thinking about who to get in touch with, I was careful to choose prudently. I made sure that I surrounded myself only with the people who were positive and who would certainly pay attention to me and not be judgemental or exacerbate any feelings of shame or guilt I may have had. This encouraged me to act positively even when I was feeling negative. It also ensured that I felt free and safe to be vulnerable and tell the truth about what I was experiencing, without fretting about being criticised, judged or told how to act. I realised that, although I was crying inside, to others I was just my normal, bubbly self; my support network held the space for me and allowed me to be me, whatever that might mean on a day-by-day basis as I recovered and healed.

Learning Point: Refuse to be isolated – surround yourself with positive supportive friends and family, not people who make you feel ashamed and guilt-stricken, people who spend time to help you moan and complain about the negatives of your past and the flaws of your ex-spouse or 'wasband' as a wonderful dear friend of mine says.

Cultivating New Friendships

Losing your social networks following the divorce or break up is inevitable; mutual family and friends often take sides and choose camps to belong to. Sometimes this can be quite disheartening and quite demoralising. Be that as it may, you must try your utmost to meet new people. Join a special interest club or network group, join a class, participate in community projects, or help out at a church, school or other community organisation.

Consider joining a support group where you are able to communicate with and help others in similar situations. Isolating yourself will only elevate your stress levels, diminish your self-esteem, lower your concentration, and hinder your work, relationships and general health. It is important that you find at least one place or forum where you are comfortable talking freely and are able to lose yourself helping others.

Coping with a break up or divorce is difficult. However, it is vital that you know (and also keep reminding yourself) that you can move ahead. I found that healing is definitely a gradual process, so be patient with yourself and take things one day at a time.

What NOT To Do!

Isolation and grief can be paralysing after a divorce but, in time, the pathos starts to ease. Each day, and bit by bit, you begin to move on. But, if you feel that you are not seeing any progress, you may be making one of the following mistakes:

1. Don't hide. Even if it is hard to discuss your emotions with others, it is vital to locate a means of doing this while you are grieving. I am a bit of a Mrs. Bucket kind of person – Mrs. Bouquet. If you live in England and watched the sitcom *Keeping up Appearances* in the 90s, you will appreciate this. However, learning to open up a bit more and sharing my vulnerabilities with people I could trust helped me immeasurably. Just by being aware that other people knew about my feelings often made me feel less isolated with my problems and fears thus assisting greatly with my healing process.

2. Do not rely on one person too much. If you burden one friend with all of your emotional issues, then they are likely to feel overwhelmed and unable to help and could even lead to you being avoided. For this reason, I made the decision to spread the discussions about the issues surrounding the divorce out among several of my closest friends. This is a wonderful strategy as it helps you get a more balanced view and potential solutions from a wider spectrum of your trusted support network.

3. Don't drown yourself in work like I did. I started to keep late hours at work because I couldn't face the realities at home. A relationship breakup or divorce can uproot almost every aspect of your existence, magnifying feelings of uncertainty, chaos and stress. Returning to a normal and balanced routine gave me a reassuring sense of normality and structure.

4. Do not make the mistake of neglecting your health. When you are in the midst of a divorce, you might be lured into doing anything to ease your feelings of loneliness and pain. However, using drugs, food or alcohol as a solution is unwise and

114

detrimental over the long term. For me it was chocolate, ice cream and shopping; trust me; both my physical and financial health began to feel the strain.

5. If you are a parent, please do not make the mistake of pressuring your children. For children, and mine were no different, the breakup can be a sad, confusing and stressful time. Allowing your emotional turmoil to take its toll on your children puts them under undue pressure, particularly because they often feel they are to blame and their confidence becomes battered. Helping your children deal with your breakup means giving them stability at home and tending to their emotional and physical needs with a positive reassuring attitude.

6. Don't confuse financial issues with emotional issues. Try not to make any major decisions straight after a separation or divorce, especially with regards to financial issues. Such decisions as selling your matrimonial home for a clean break or taking out significant loans to finance your business or even leaving your job are big Nos Nos at this time. Make sure to wait until you are feeling less emotional so that you are in a better frame of mind to make more informed and better decisions.

7. Do not deny your part in the break up. As much as we all like to believe it was all his or her fault, even if that were true, try and take a step back and observe the bigger picture. What contribution did you make to the relationship's problems? Accept your responsibility, learn from it, forgive yourself, and move on. The worst thing you could do would be to take unresolved baggage into your new life.

8. Do not stop being active and sociable. When you are encountering the stress of a break up, good habits quickly fall by the way-side. I know I often found myself indulging in my favourite junk foods and sitting glued in front of the television. There were even times when I would not eat at all but would down several ice cold bottles of Coke. My dentist was always happy to see me; I wonder why? I often found myself bursting with short-lived spurts of energy then I would become lethargic

so much so that I found exercising more difficult to schedule and I encountered frequent episodes of insomnia.

9. This is a biggie; in times of emotional vulnerability, please resist seeking solace in things that are out of alignment with your values. Some people turn to fraudulent clairvoyants and mediums for guidance, or bizarre religious cults. Some even resort to drugs and alcohol abuse. Do not allow yourself to be part of this statistic; stick with the people you know. If you are a person of faith, stick to your faith. Seek the help of reputable professional counsellors, divorce coaches and mentors if you need help outside of your circle of friends and/or faith.

10. Another biggie: do not believe your life is over. Although you have been through a painful divorce or relationship breakdown and are now single, you are still part of the human race. I found it quite a liberating feeling once I realised that I still had a life to live with the advantage now of not being either stuck in a dead-end relationship as I was before or even being dead.

11. When you are recovering from the trauma and pain of a divorce or long term relationship breakdown, one sure NO NO that you cannot afford to do is to have sex with your ex-partner. You must ensure you stop all forms of physical contact completely. The pain of withdrawal will be difficult especially at the times of the month when you get sexual urges, remembering how it was when you were together or how it could have been. Remember, you need to have your wits about you at all times. There is a famous biblical quotation that I found particularly helpful to me at these times:

> **"As a dog eats its own vomit,**
> **so fools recycle silliness."**
> **Proverbs 26:11**

Do not be fooled or deceived by those stories that you may hear about needing to be nice to the 'wasband' or the ex. If you are fortunate to be on cordial terms, please remember that the niceness must not include any physical contact. Engaging in sex with your ex will give you both mixed messages. It is indeed a terrible road to take, can be very devastating to your emotional state and says a lot about your negative self-esteem.

It is crucial that we are honest with ourselves and try to analyse our own behaviour and choices objectively. We will then get to know where we made errors and make better decisions next time. I know you do not want to recycle the mistakes or silliness of the past.

Overcoming Guilt

If you are experiencing guilt following your break up, the other feelings might be intensified. Although some people feel sadness, pain, depression, anger and much more – I personally felt a whole lot worse since I had guilt eating away at me. For me, being a woman of faith, I felt as if I had disappointed God, disappointed myself and disappointed my family. Everyone looked up to me and I was the first divorced person in a family known for successful and long marriages. This may not be your problem, but I do know guilt comes in different guises, so my question is what does the guilt mean and what can we do about this? This chapter talks about feeling guilt after our break up, what this means and ways to use our guilt in a productive way.

Generally, we experience guilt whenever we do something amiss and, with regards to divorce, whenever we did something to our ex-spouse that may have contributed to the divorce or was the entire reason for the divorce. For me, this made it very hard to deal with the guilt and carry on, but remember, nothing is impossible if you only believe.

The very first thing we must do is think about the main reason we are feeling guilty. What did we do or say that is causing us to feel guilty now? Think about the one thing you did and acknowledge it. This is essential – you will need to simply accept the truth that you did whatever you did to be able to move ahead together with your life.

Next, you will need to understand that everyone makes mistakes and that you are human. Be generous to yourself and try to split the guilt evenly with your ex, regardless of what anyone else might have to say.

Now you will need to take control over the matter that you are feeling guilty about and utilise it to enhance your existence. Maybe you didn't have sufficient communication in your marriage which contributed to its downfall; maybe sexual relations broke down after the birth of your fifth child, you just did not have the urge and your husband started cheating on you. Regardless of what it was, recognise it and make a move to focus on it. For example, you could access some counselling or therapy to show you how to become more communicative to prevent this from occurring again, maybe there is an underlying medical issue regarding the loss of your libido after child birth or maybe it's post-natal depression; contact your GP to investigate further. The end result is for you to come out of it with an excellent bill of health.

For me, I utilised my guilty and negative emotions to enhance my own future by turning the events that led to the breakdown of my marriage on their head. I have always been a person who makes excuses for a loved one's bad behaviour, compromising where I shouldn't. In order to avoid this type of behaviour going forward, I have put things in place where I take responsibility for my actions only and not someone else's, this includes my children. This is because as a single parent I was beginning to see a repeat of certain patterns of my behaviour where I would take on responsibility to justify something my children did. It really is all about valuing and loving yourself.

I also discovered that, try as I might, I cannot truly control another person's behaviour. I can put boundaries in place, but I must not take on full responsibility for unacceptable or bad behaviour of a loved one, be it my children or my spouse. I now include this discovery as a foundational block in my divorce and abuse recovery coaching by helping women to truly understand that we cannot control other people's behaviour. Nor should we try or take on the blame for when it is wrong.

For example, perhaps your ex-spouse was indulging in behaviour you found unacceptable. I am talking about behaviour that was having a negative impact on not just you, but on your children too. Please understand that you cannot force him to change his behaviour, and I am sure many of you reading this now may have found this out the hard way while you were still married, like I did. However, at the same time, you shouldn't just accept it either.

It is all about setting clear unambiguous boundaries. This is especially true if you have children from the marriage or relationship and exceptionally useful to learn for when you go into a new marriage or relationship, should you choose to do so.

I know first-hand after my own experience that establishing or setting new personal boundaries are extremely powerful and important especially after a divorce or relationship break up for several reasons.

Firstly, they serve as barriers to protect your self-esteem. They are also tools for establishing limits with others and communicating that you won't tolerate certain behaviours. Those without personal boundaries commonly end up in less than ideal situations and relationships. This is the same whether you are divorced or not.

Without setting boundaries or limits, you become a victim to the whims of those around you. Personal boundaries are about respecting yourself and demanding respect from others.

Zina, what is a boundary? I hear you ask.

A boundary is a conscious decision about what you will and will not allow into your life. It is a metaphorical line we draw around ourselves to protect our physical and emotional wellbeing. Boundaries can be spoken or unspoken.

A very good example of a clear and unambiguous boundary is that we will not allow another person to hit us. This means: **If you hit me, I will not remain in this relationship.**

Having clear boundaries communicates a message to the people in our lives. Setting boundaries gives us freedom because we are not constantly trying to second guess what we will or will not accept. Setting boundaries ensures we avoid sending mixed, unclear and inconsistent messages.

Three key action points involved in setting boundaries include:

♥ ***Follow Through:*** Upholding the boundary when it has been violated. Parents are often guilty of not doing this. I know I am especially with regard to my youngest daughter. What I have learnt, and am still learning, is that when we don't follow through, the boundary can be likened to an empty threat. The person, either your spouse or child or both, realises we were not serious with the setting of that boundary and sadly the negative behaviour continues.

♥ ***Be Fearless:*** Do not be fearful of the consequences of following through on a boundary violation. For instance, if your husband hits you, don't start being afraid of how he will survive if you call the police or of how the children will cope or worry about what the neighbours will say. You must be fearless and decisive.

♥ ***Never Blame Yourself:*** Many times we let ourselves believe that we are somehow responsible and therefore feel guilty about following through. This often happens when your child acts out at school. You want to impose sanctions but feel guilty that the actions could attributed to the breakdown of your marriage. Sometimes your ex or your children might use manipulation to feed that belief when you attempt to follow through with boundary rules.

By not having effective boundaries in place we are inadvertently and unconsciously conveying that we do not love ourselves enough to value our own emotional needs. I discovered that it is crucial that we become unapologetic and audacious in honouring, respecting and upholding our boundaries so that we do not become helpless in condoning or enabling repeated unacceptable behaviour.

How Do We Set Effective Boundaries?

Is it Clear – The best place to start is by being really clear about the boundaries you want to set and the reasons why you want to set them. What is their purpose? As part of this, it might be a good idea to also think about how each unacceptable behaviour is impacting your physical or emotional wellbeing so as to set a boundary that communicates that you can no longer tolerate that behaviour.

Is it Enforceable – Ensure you communicate the consequences for violating a boundary and the steps you will be taking to enforce it. Setting a boundary without being prepared to enforce it communicates that we do not follow through or honour ourselves thereby giving express permission for the unacceptable behaviour to persist.

Ask Yourself What's Worse – Facing up to the fear of upholding your boundary or continuing to tolerate and therefore enable the intolerable behaviour?

The Boundary is for YOU not HIM – Understand that when you set a boundary you are not asking the other person to change their behaviour – they can behave however they want to. It is not about making a threat that says: "Do this, or else."

In setting the boundary you get to decide how you are going to respond to that behaviour – i.e. "If you choose to do X, I will choose to do Y."

Make a Commitment to Yourself – Enforcing your boundaries is a commitment you make to yourself. It is about taking care of your own needs. It is an act of self-love and self-care.

So my question to you as you read this is, "do you value yourself enough to set and uphold clear boundaries?"

Exercise 6. **Boundaries**

Here's a bit of light restorative home work:

What challenges have you faced in setting and enforcing boundaries with your ex-spouse or anyone else in your life? How did you overcome them? Be true to you; if you have not set any boundaries yet, don't beat yourself up. There is no better time than the present. Start now! Go on, have a go at committing to and writing some boundaries down now.

_____

_____

_____

_____

_____

_____

_____

_____

_____

_____

_____

Coming back to the issue of guilt, no matter what you may or may not have done to contribute to the breakdown of your marriage, there is a method of learning from it to make yourself better and much more knowledgeable. Guilt is never a nice feeling, however it does not need to be a negative thing. Utilise it, as I did, to your advantage for a much better future.

122

Chapter 4.

LEARNING TO LAUGH AGAIN

Adam and Eve had an ideal marriage.
He didn't have to hear about all the men she could have married and
she didn't have to hear about the way his mother cooked. ☺

Smiling can influence and reflect our moods. Additionally, it may help us cope with the complex and difficult world we reside in and adjust to the issues we face, like the challenge of starting our lives again following divorce. Laughing plays an important part in the social arena and helps develop social support. It is, therefore, a good policy to adopt laughter throughout our lives generally, but after a break up we need to start instituting it straight away.

Why do we smile?

Since we are social animals, we acquire positive support from showing our happier moods through smiling. The smile is recognized as welcoming and we anticipate an optimistic response from a person who is smiling.

Smiling can impact your mood.

Studies show that people can make a difference to our emotions by smiling on purpose. We all know smiling occurs spontaneously whenever we experience happiness; however, it appears that the reverse could also be true. This close link between mood and smiling may be utilized to our benefit by suppressing the negative emotions we feel following a difficult event like divorce. Warm, genuine smiles are the very best to affect our moods.

Smiling is usually the very last thing that most people feel like doing following a divorce. Yet, making an effort to smile might be exactly the thing you need. Laughing and smiling, but not over-doing it, have already been proven to create a beneficial effect on mood. Improving my moods allowed me to see my difficulties, as well as my situation, in another light and provided me with the energy to deal with them and thrive. According to many studies, laughter is even stronger than smiling in elevating mood.

Strengthen your health.

The more you laugh, the less frequently you'll be sick. Studies have shown that laughing strengthens the immune system. It also lowers your blood pressure, which is great for your heart and brain. It's possible that laughter can lower your medical expenses.

Humour and end of life care.

Studies show that humour appears in the care in hospices for patients who are terminally ill and seventy percent of this humour was initiated by the patients. Divorce is classed as the 2nd most stressful lifestyle event after bereavement. Humour ought to be among the tools we use to cope with that stress. Searching for the funny and the ridiculous in the divorce and healing process can help speed up our adjustment to our fresh lives.

Strengthen your relationships.

Is it possible to have a relationship that wouldn't benefit from your sense of humour? Of course not! I firmly believe that laughing together brings you closer together. You will find that as you do, your relationships with your neighbours, friends, family, and co-workers will benefit a great deal from your ability to laugh and appreciate the lighter side of life. This is especially useful in your divorce recovery and reinvention journey.

Reduce stress.

Daily life after divorce is stressful. There are many ways to relieve stress, but few feel as good as laughing. With a good sense of humour, it's easy to find reasons to laugh about life. A good laugh will allow you to forget about your challenges for a little while.

Uplift your mood.

Trust me, it really feels good to laugh, and the good feelings can last for hours afterwards. A well-developed sense of humour can redirect your focus from the negative happenings in your life to something more enjoyable.

Increase your intelligence.

At the very least, you'll learn more easily. This is a good benefit, especially if you are thinking of going back to school to retrain and change your career after divorce. A study demonstrated that laughing stimulates the learning centres of the brain. Stimulating those areas on a regular basis is believed to enhance the ability to learn new information. Who knows? Laughing might help you get that scholarship into Oxford, Cambridge or Harvard 20 or 30 years on.

Laughter is the greatest medicine.

If you've watched the 1998 film Patch Adams, a semi-biographical comedy-drama starring Robin Williams based on the life story of Dr. Hunter "Patch" Adams and his book, *Gesundheit: Good Health is a Laughing Matter,* by Adams and Maureen Mylander, you will know how humour could be included in therapy. Today, humour as a coping tool has been mixed into psychological therapies and there is an acknowledgement that humour is a beneficial way of adapting to testing circumstances. The Bible tells us in Proverbs 17:22:

"A merry heart does good, like medicine, but a broken spirit dries the bones".

Laughter has the ability to help us adjust to tough situations like divorce in 2 ways:

♥ It distances us psychologically from the negative event

♥ It encourages social support from other people

The first way reduces the negative impact this event might have on our lives and the second gives us social support to supplement the coping skills we now have.

Smile and the world smiles with you.

As it happens, this saying has lots of truth to it. Try utilising the ability of laughter and humour to help you cope with the hard circumstances you are confronted by. Try, also, surrounding yourself with happy, positive people, because feelings may also be spread from group laughter.

Laughing is good for you. **Your sense of humour impacts your health, mood, social life, and those around you.** When you're in a bad mood, it negatively impacts others. Your smiling, happy face and mood are uplifting and brighten the moods of those around you. They say that laughter is the best medicine. Now you have a better idea why that statement is true. Find the humour in life and keep your mood light. There are no benefits to expecting the worst and experiencing negative moods.

Spend time with others who enjoy laughing. Make it a point to enjoy funny movies or watch your favourite comedians. Your laughter helps you and those around you. Feel free to laugh more.

As you may have gathered, I really believe in the power of happiness and laughter. I love laughing, I really do. Happiness has always been my default state, even during my traumatic and painful divorce. I recall speaking with my best friend the other day and she reminded me how she is always amazed at my innate ability to uncover humour even in the most mundane things. She said, "Zina, you are so funny, you are even able to laugh in the midst of tears and sadness." Which is true!

Even when my daughters were younger and I would be in the midst of some fierce disciplinary show down, I would suddenly remember something funny and burst into fits of laughter or would make some silly analogy in a bid to drive my point home My daughters would look at me strangely, thinking "Mum, did you really just say that?" Too late to recover my stern pose, we would then all fall down into a heap as peals of laughter would sail off into the atmosphere. Family happiness was restored which normally meant the end of my parental rant.

My happiness and humour is entwined into everything I am and do; even my faith. Here are two declarations I developed and have reproduced for you. I have modified them slightly into personal exercises you may find useful especially if you are a woman of faith and happiness is not your default state.

Exercise 7. **Happiness Declarations**

Each morning, stand in front of your bathroom mirror and make a point of making these declarations:

- ♥ My faith makes me smile.

- ♥ My spiritual beliefs build a strong foundation for my happiness. Faith allows me to feel secure, so I can relax and enjoy life.

- ♥ I learn to regard myself and others with compassion. I try to see the humorous side of the errors that we all make.

- ♥ My faith allows me to share fun times with those around me. I connect with others who share my convictions. We exchange laughter and support.

- ♥ I become more tolerant. It is easier for me to forgive others, even when my feelings are hurt. I can move passed anger and sadness. Affectionate feelings are quickly restored. Arguments give way to more pleasant interactions.

- ♥ Having faith puts things in perspective and helps me understand what really matters. I act responsibly without taking life too seriously.

♥ There are many ways for me to use my faith to express my happiness.

♥ Prayer becomes a warm conversation with the Divine. It is okay for me to describe a funny experience or pour out my heart. Gentle meditation allows me to tackle sensitive topics without feeling threatened or overwhelmed. Praise and Worship songs lift my spirits.

♥ I remind myself that others may be influenced by my mood. When I am cheerful, I share the benefits of my faith with others. I socialise with the people I pray with.

♥ Today, I choose to rejoice in the good feelings that arise from practicing my faith. My tensions dissolve into laughter and contentment.

Self-Reflection Questions:

Why does humour strengthen my faith?

_____

_____

How can faith help me to smile during stressful times?

_____

_____

Each morning, stand upright in front of your bathroom mirror and make a point of making these declarations

♥ I love to laugh.

♥ Laughter enhances my physical, mental, and spiritual wellbeing. I develop my sense of humour and discover opportunities to laugh more often.

♥ Laughter releases my inhibitions. I stop taking myself so seriously. I give myself permission to look silly and have a good time. I feel more open. I unleash my creativity.

♥ Laughter draws me closer to others. Sharing joy strengthens my relationships. I am grateful to my family and friends when they cheer me up. I try to spread those good feelings around by staying upbeat.

♥ Laughter helps me to learn. Dry facts come to life when I connect them with an interesting story. When I am amused, I can face my mistakes and analyse them so I know what changes to make.

♥ I laugh to minimise irritations.

♥ I laugh to promote healing. I turn my tears into laughter by focusing on the comical aspects of the situation. When I relax, I can think logically and see events from a different perspective that allows me to grow.

♥ I laugh to overcome challenges. When I am struggling with a difficult task, I turn it into a game. I look for ways to have fun while cleaning the garage, changing the light bulbs, fixing a leak or helping my children with their homework.

♥ I laugh at myself. I acknowledge my own eccentricities.

♥ Today, I bring more laughter into my life. I lighten up and look for the humour in each experience.

Self-Reflection Questions:

Why is laughter therapeutic?

_____

_____

What is one funny thing that happened to me this week?

_____

_____

How does laughter encourage mindfulness?

_____

_____

Chapter 5.
DEALING WITH REJECTION

Speak out. It's good to talk!

Rejection is one of the prime feelings experienced when experiencing a divorce. It is important to not become too isolated but to seek out trusted friends and family you can talk to. You might not feel like talking to anyone, even if you are a chatty person like I am. I get that because there was a period I just couldn't bring myself to talk about what I was feeling or what I was going through. I didn't know if I could ever trust again after being betrayed by marriage. I was absolutely petrified of being ridiculed or appearing weak and vulnerable. I am a talker, however all I wanted to do was to be mute, hide my real feelings and be left to curl up under my duvet and disappear forever.

If this is how you are feeling, I get that. Perhaps you are going through an entire selection of powerful emotions: anger, sadness, hurt, concern about an unknown future, confusion concerning the numerous decisions you have to make, loneliness and a feeling of failure at your broken dreams and plans. Again, if this is how you are feeling, I get that.

However, how you decide to handle this journey is pivotal to the remainder of your life. If you bottle up these feelings because you find yourself unable to cope with the pain and do not speak out, ultimately you could become very bitter and extremely unhappy for many years to come.

I strongly encourage you to speak out. Talking to others will help you in no small way to deal with potential bitterness and persistent anger. "Reciprocation of confidences" with trusted friends and family becomes a chance for you talk freely through your divorce to re-examine your abilities, assets and dreams and help make the changes essential for a brand new, full and rewarding life. This is basically the UK's British Telecom's foundation branding which started in 2000 using four memorable simple words that we all use still use today: "IT'S GOOD TO TALK".

It is Good to Talk! Yeah! Yeah! Zina, I grew up watching the BT adverts with Bob Hoskins. But how do I apply this to my life?

Here are a few steps you can take:

♥ **Speak with somebody you trust**. Speaking with a relative or good friend can provide you with an outlet for the frustration and anger. Take care not to burden your kids with any of these feelings. Make sure you can trust the individual to keep your secrets so you feel liberated to share your deepest concerns. As I mentioned earlier, I personally found that someone who has also experienced a separation or divorce was the most appropriate type of person to offer support as long as they have a positive perspective.

♥ **Keep the lines of communication open with your kids.** They have to be aware that they're not losing the support and love of either parent, and they aren't accountable for your divorce or separation. I spoke frankly to my daughters, my amazing princesses, about our new living arrangements and found that this helped considerably. Make and keep realistic promises. And don't overly confide with them about your feelings concerning the divorce.

♥ **Get specialised help when it is needed.** You will face many legal and emotional issues alongside divorce proceedings, and you will probably need expert advice. For legal matters, seek the aid of a family solicitor. If you are going through immense emotional turmoil, your GP can assist you in finding a counsellor and a divorce recovery coach. You may even find it is useful to have a chat with your pastor or reverend. The secret is to use these services and disregard the need to 'tough it out' by yourself.

♥ **Search for support in your community.** There might be workshops and self-help groups in your local area which could assist you in this difficult time. I found that becoming a hermit actually increased my stress, dented my focus and negatively impacted my professional life, friendships and vitality. So, don't hesitate to get outside help as often as you need it.

Experiencing a divorce is always very hard, regardless of why it is happening. It can turn everything on its head and make normal everyday tasks a challenge to complete. Don't bottle up your feelings – talk to others. This way you will still be capable of getting through your work day and staying productive.

Remember: It Is Good To Talk! And when you are able to talk you will find that you are able to laugh again too.

27th October 2011

Dear Father God, it is me again.

I know you see all things and can see me as I write in my beloved Journie. Please help me Lord. It seems to be getting better, but sometimes I get so confused. Show me what to do. Lead me through this painful process of rejection and bring me out the other side. I pray - I trust in You and I am not afraid. Thank You Father, that You are always there for me. Amen.

Studies suggest that in an estimated 70% of divorces, an ex-spouse left to be with someone else. One thing is for sure; no matter how emotionally resilient you may be, being rejected intensifies particular emotions or feelings. For instance, feeling insecure, experiencing low self-esteem, shame, feeling like a failure, a complete loser, and/or feelings of negative self-worth.

How rejection fans the flames of insecurity.

In the event that you have felt poorly treated in past relationships – whatever age you happened to be and regardless of the reason – a sense of rejection could be fuelling your belief that you're not worth having that special someone.

It can also be that you have felt rejected over sometime – perhaps in the bedroom, or perhaps by your ex-spouse treating you with contempt.

If that sense of worthlessness does not pass, make sure that you locate some specialised help. I personally found that professional Christian counselling in my local church certainly helped me to 'find myself' again and taught me how to approach rejection, since it is an element of life we all have to face at some point no matter what age we are.

If you want spiritual or psychological counselling, seek somebody out and review how the counselling sessions might help you.

How to deal with rejection and build your self-esteem.

Coping with rejection could be very difficult, but finding methods to handle rejection is important so you will get through it. Suggestions about how to approach rejection will include techniques for rebuilding your self-esteem.

Below I have listed some of the options that proved invaluable for me when I was at my lowest ebb:

♥ Participate in activities – mental or physical – that enable you to feel like you have achieved something.

♥ Make a summary of the goals you wish to accomplish.

♥ Include small, medium and large goals – allow the mind to operate freely

♥ Get started instantly with a few of the smaller goals – this is widely regarded as an effective way of dealing with rejection.

♥ Motivate yourself by visualising what you will feel, see and hear when you reach your goal. Do this frequently and allow it to be the last thought you have before you drift off to sleep. Concentrate on these goals in the event that you awaken during the night time!

Stay Active!

Make sure, after your divorce, to keep yourself busy and to treat yourself from time to time. I found that doing activities that made me feel positive about myself or spending time with the people I love – my family and friends – set the stage for moving forward to new relationships, or as some would say, 'a new start' in life.

Re-evaluate your existence and rediscover who you are and the things you like. Develop new relationships and new areas of your life as these are the things you need. You are independent now so begin doing all the things that interested you, but stopped doing in your marriage, or look for new methods to occupy your time.

Emotions are not wrong or right, they are just... emotions. After divorce, you may be reminded of the negative and positive times that you have had. When taking trips down memory lane be honest with yourself. Do not blame yourself, get active support, spend some time on your self-development, pamper yourself and move on. Move ahead targeting the goals you had previously along with new goals, letting go of goals you had with your partner since your existence has been redefined.

Finally, at this point, you now know a bit more about how to approach rejection. Choose for yourself what you ought to do next. Begin by creating an action plan specifying dates and times.

Very often self-esteem is used interchangeably and seen as a synonym for self-worth and vice versa. So I will touch briefly on what self-worth is and why it is also important to you during and after divorce.

The dictionary defines self-worth as "the sense of one's own value or worth as a person."

Happiness after divorce becomes quite elusive without restoring a sense of self-worth. The question is, if you're not happy with yourself, how can you be happy about life in general? Self-worth is about believing that you have value as a person, divorced or not. It's not about how you compare to others. It's your belief in your intrinsic value as a human being. It is accepting that you matter and that you are important. We're all important. Some of us just require a little more convincing than others.

A good place to start is by acknowledging and honouring our strengths, qualities and accomplishments. But that is not all. It is about recognising the treasure that you are. It is about owning your immense value within your sphere of influence. Self-worth is about who you are and not what you do or have done.

You are worth more than rubies.
– Proverbs 31:10

Dr. Kristin Neff one of the world's leading experts on self-compassion, argues that there is a problem with society's focus on high self-esteem. "The problem is that this focus involves measuring oneself against others, rather than paying attention to one's intrinsic value," says Dr. Neff. In this sense, searching for self-worth by constantly comparing our self-worth vs. self-esteem to others means to always be fighting a losing battle. As Dr. Neff says, "There is always someone richer, more attractive or more successful than we are. And even when we do manage to feel self-esteem for one golden moment, we can't hold on to it. Our sense of self-worth bounces around like a ping-pong ball, rising and falling in lock-step with our latest success or failure."

As mindfulness expert Dr. Donna Rockwell points out, we are all unique and that, in and of itself, gives each of us inherent value. According to Dr. Firestone, "We shouldn't be rating ourselves, we should just be ourselves."

How to Restore Your Self-Worth?

The first step in restoring self-worth is to stop comparing yourself to others who may still be married and evaluating your marriage based on theirs. It is at this stage that you really need to challenge your inner critic or your negative self-talk which might be silently taunting you like mine did to me saying "everyone else is a better wife than I ever was".

The critical inner voice or gremlin as I like to call it is like a relentless nagging and disgusting coach in our heads filling us up with destructive thoughts towards ourselves or others. Challenge that foul inner critic and instead see yourself like God sees you, for who you really are, bluntly refusing to take on its negative suggestions and point of view about ourselves. The next step in restoring your true sense of self-worth is by practicing self-compassion. According to Dr Kirstin Neff, Self-compassion is the practice of treating yourself with the same kindness and compassion as you would treat a friend or family member. This involves taking on what Dr. Dan Siegel describes as the "COAL" attitude, which means being Curious, Open, Accepting, and Loving toward yourself and your experiences rather than being self-critical.

There are three steps to practicing self-compassion:

1. Acknowledge and notice your suffering.

2. Be kind and caring in response to suffering.

3. Remember that imperfection is part of the human experience and something we all share.

You add meaning to your life by taking part in activities that you feel are important and this is another great way to build self-worth.

Silence your critical inner voice and stop comparing yourself to others, so that you can begin to get an enhanced feeling for your own self-worth. By pursuing activities that are meaningful to you and acting in line with your own personal beliefs, you foster a positive sense of self as a worthwhile person in the world.

Exercise 8. **Self-worth Rebuilding**

Begin rebuilding and restoring your self-worth by listing below all the strengths and great qualities you have. Have close friends and family help by asking them to tell you what they see that is valuable in you. You are a desirable person.

Strengths and Qualities Inventory

What I am good at?

_____

_____

What do I like about my appearance?

_____

_____

Compliments I have received:

_____

_____

_____

Challenges I have overcome:

_____

_____

_____

How I have helped others:

_____

_____

_____

Times I have made other people happy:

_____

_____

What are my five key values?

_____

_____

What makes me so unique?

_____

_____

Five words describing your strengths

_____

_____

Five transferable skills

_____

_____

Five qualities others use to describe you

_____

_____

Three things you are passionate about

_____

_____

What are five of your dislikes?

_____

_____

Name three hobbies

_____

_____

My ultimate dream if money was no object:

_____

_____

How would you like to be remembered?

_____

_____

Chapter 6.

HOW TO SEE CLEARLY FOR YOUR FUTURE

One of the biggest gifts of divorce, yes I said gifts, is that it can become an opportunity to develop clarity and focus for your future new reality. With the right support, you are better equipped and empowered to navigate past the emotions in your new life. In turn, you will find, like I did, that that you become more decisive and the mental barriers that may have been keeping you stuck are removed. Through this process you are able to finally become clear about what you want and you will learn what you need to do to move forward.

Here are 25 Clarity questions that form part of my *Believe and Live Again! Clarity and Focus Coaching* programme. I have formulated these questions to help you gain more clarity in finding your 'why' and discovering your passion and purpose. Using your note pad, journal or mobile tablet device, I strongly recommend that you have a go at answering these questions. You will be amazed at how the haze of divorce begins to rise and, just like Jonny Nash sang, you too with a spring in your step will begin to sing, "I Can See Clearly Now the "Haze" has gone.

I Can See Clearly Now, the Rain is Gone

— Johnny Nash (1972)

I can see clearly now, the rain is gone
I can see all obstacles in my way
Gone are the dark clouds that had me blind
It's gonna be a bright (bright), bright (bright)
Sun shiny day

I think I can make it now, the pain is gone
All of the bad feelings have disappeared
Here is the rainbow I've been prayin' for
It's gonna be a bright (bright), bright (bright)
Sun shiny day

Look all around, there's nothin' but blue skies
Look straight ahead, nothin' but blue skies
I can see clearly now the rain has gone
I can see all obstacles in my way
Gone are the dark clouds that had me blind
It's gonna be a bright (bright), bright (bright)
Sun shiny day

Exercise 9. **Clarity and Focus Pathway Tool**

Clarity questions

Who are you?

_____

_____

_____

What are you passionate about?

_____

_____

_____

What is your ideal career?

_____

_____

_____

What are the achievements you are most proud of?

_____

_____

_____

What are you most grateful for in life?

_____

_____

_____

_____

_____

What are the most important things to you in life?

_____

_____

_____

How would you describe yourself?

_____

_____

_____

What are your values? What do you represent? What do you want to embody?

_____

_____

_____

Look at your life now. Are you living the life of your dreams?

_____

_____

_____

If you had one year left to live, what would you do?

_____

_____

_____

If you had one month left to live, what would you do?

_____

_____

_____

If you had one week left to live, what would you do?

_____

_____

_____

_____

If you had one day left to live, what would you do?

_____

_____

_____

_____

If you had an hour left to live, what would you do?

_____

_____

_____

_____

If you had one minute left to live, what would you do?

_____

_____

_____

What would you do today if there were no more tomorrows?

_____

_____

_____

What are the biggest things you've learned in life to date? What advice would you give to yourself 3 years ago?

_____

_____

_____

_____

_____

_____

Where are you living right now – the past, future or present?

_____

_____

_____

Are you living your life to the fullest right now? What are your dreams?

_____

_____

_____

What is your purpose in life? Why do you exist? What is your mission?

_____

_____

_____

Are you putting any parts of your life on hold? ... Why?

_____

_____

_____

How can you make your life more meaningful, starting today?

_____

_____

_____

_____

Who are the 5 people you spend the most time with?

_____

_____

Are these people enabling you or holding you back?

_____

_____

_____

List your top 10 goals.

_____

_____

_____

_____

_____

_____

_____

_____

_____

_____

Chapter 7.

FINANCIAL PLANNING FOR THE FUTURE

If you have been through divorce, you will, without doubt, have many problems to be worried about such as your own future security, the welfare of your family and kids and anything else that accompanies this type of stressful time.

Clearly, a relationship breakdown may have a significant impact on your finances. You will likely be bothered with numerous financial problems, which can easily be managed through effective financial plans.

Financial plans will assist with your break up by clarifying where your money stands before you split, and what effect the resolutions may have in your future.

Obviously, if both sides know where they stand with their money, they might have a much better possibility of reaching an agreement without unnecessary conflict.

Here are a few example situations where extensive financial planning might help within a divorce:

Your own future life style

The primary aim of financial planning is to assess your present and future lifestyle. An extensive analysis will highlight the impact of losing or gaining income and assets, and whether this will alter your present or future finances.

The household home

There are lots of possible resolutions to the issue of what may occur to the family home on divorce. You might decide that certain parties will remain in your house, or it may be put on the property market and the sale funds split between the parties. If a home loan has been taken, this will further add to the problem.

If you wish to keep the home, you may want to discover if you are able to afford a brand new mortgage on the house in your sole name; alternately, even if you don't keep the marital home, you will still have to know if you are able to afford accommodation elsewhere.

In some instances, the one who leaves can still have a financial stake in your home until it is sold later on. Financial plans can enable you to work out what this signifies for the future.

Maintenance for children

It is quite common for maintenance to be paid following a break up. Financial plans can enable you to accurately establish the amount required, and what this income or expense means for your life style. You don't need to visit court to determine just how much should be paid. Great financial planning can assist both parties in reaching a quick resolution as to a suitable amount of monetary support.

Pensions

This is yet another area that will need financial thought after divorce. The pensions of either side could be a significant asset, and it is common for these to be shared on a divorce, with one side obtaining a portion of the pension of the other side.

Financial plans are required for both parties: the individual losing the pension assets must know very well what they have to do to recuperate their lost retirement income; the receiving party must know how the pension assets might be of use in planning their future. They should also administer these assets using investment management.

Hopefully, all of this has shown the importance of financial planning before and after a divorce.

Chapter 8.
YOUR HEALTH IS PARAMOUNT

Those amongst us who are divorced could suffer 20% more from chronic health problems, such as cardiovascular disease, diabetes or cancer, than people who are married. This statistic originates from research published in the September 2009 publication of the *Journal of Health & Social Behaviour.*

The study of 8,652 women and men within their fifties and early sixties in America discovered that the physical stresses of losing a marriage continues for a long time even once the emotional ailments have eased. While this does not imply that couples should remain in an unhappy marriage no matter what, it indicates that the soon-to-be and recently divorced have to be particularly vigilant about stress management and exercise.

People can suffer enormous stress as their broken marriages grind to a halt. Aside from the numerous negative feelings concerning the split like fear and anger, further concerns include the search for new accommodation, financial resources that need to be stretched, the connection with family and friends that is lost or strained, broken sleep, lower quality diet and lesser exercise, which causes an unhealthy lifestyle that contributes to stress levels. Divorce is among the most intense stressors.

To lessen that stress, it is wise to select a non-adversarial method of divorce, like Family Mediation or Collaborative Practice. Not only will this approach assist you in reaching reasonable settlements, it may also be healthier for you personally than the usual adversarial positional Divorce Court hearings.

But away from divorce courts you, nevertheless, still need to be good to yourself by developing habits that lower your stress. They include:

- ♥ Ensuring you focus on your emotional needs
- ♥ Learning to LOVE You
- ♥ Keeping in good physical shape
- ♥ Taking part in activities which will stimulate you physically and emotionally
- ♥ Not worrying about the issues that you are unable to control
- ♥ Giving yourself space to feel
- ♥ Focussing your expectations
- ♥ Giving yourself room to make choices
- ♥ Scheduling time for fun
- ♥ And generally loosening up

When experiencing a divorce, your whole life will feel the impact. When I experienced my own divorce, I found myself questioning my entire view of who I was and how I had opted to spend my life. In addition, there were the legal and financial ramifications of the divorce to mentally and emotionally process.

Booking appointments with your local GP and having frequent check-ups can help stem off illnesses due to the strain that accompanies divorce. For example, if you've got a history of high blood pressure, it seems sensible to make certain that the physical and emotional strain you are experiencing throughout your divorce does not exacerbate the issue, does it not?

The research above clearly highlights that a divorce could be harmful to your well-being. But by looking after yourself, by concentrating on keeping active and healthier, by continuing forward without getting stuck in what's gone before, and by selecting a process like collaborative practice (that targets settlement and reduces conflict), you will be able to minimise the damaging after-effects of divorce and move ahead with life.

Chapter 9.
A GREAT TIME FOR CHANGE

"Progress is impossible without change,
and those who cannot change their minds cannot change anything".
– George Bernard Shaw

Divorce is really a major life change that can leave an individual reeling. I found that suddenly being by myself to cope with problems like money, kids, career changes, and downsizing the family home was too overwhelming to handle alone. Once I had come to terms with this though, I made a point of kick-starting my life and making some changes using the following steps:

Define a brand new relationship together with your ex for the kids

Your old relationship was as a couple; your relationship now should be as common allies for your kids, if you are fortunate.

Speak to your children

Divorce can create serious emotional wounds in kids. This is especially so if the marriage was a toxic one and the divorce exceptionally acrimonious. Speak with your children about what are you doing, what they are feeling and how things can get better. Involve them. I found that once they were involved, they were able to do things to help with the transition; it provided them with a sense of power.

Create a life plan

Assess your circumstances financially; look at your resources to see what your choices are when it comes to housing, jobs and finances; in fact don't just map out new goals for your financial future but also envision new goals and create a plan covering the new chapter of your entire life.

Select a support squad

Ask for help, shout for it if you need to. People like being asked for guidance. It is a gift for them to be able to be there for you personally. Produce a support team made up from a selection of your core and closest friends who will not mind offering you professional guidance, on-going inspiration and emotional support. They understand that you are not the very first person to undergo this and therefore will not judge you.

Gather your resources and assets around you

Do all you can to program yourself for success. Discover what your strengths and skills are and concentrate on them to greatly help move you in a brand new and positive direction. Remember that you will create the outcomes in life that you think you deserve.

Actively seek 'Me' time

Make it a priority to become a little selfish and find time simply for you. Get involved in a new activity, begin exercising or re-start an old pastime you had forgotten about.

Create your dream home

It's not the end of the world if you need to change houses. Realise that you, as well as your children, are likely to create new memories there and that is why it is a dream home.

Find your authentic self

While you may no longer be one half of a couple, you are still a 100% unique individual. Discover that person again and take steps to reconnect with your feminine power and sense of self.

Find your passion – it's a time to be creative

What things will cause you to be excited about getting out of bed every day? Be creative. Discover your hidden talents, set targets and goals. When you focus on the better things that you have going for you, the trauma caused by divorce can be drastically reduced.

At this time, developing your creativity is the best thing you can do. Many people are conscious of the "gift" they possess, that thing they love to do. Whatever you love, whether it is singing, sports, crafting, painting, dancing, and no matter how crazy other people may seem to think of it, if it brings you joy, it's time to start that particular activity again. Although in many it is hidden, every single person has a creative side.

- ♥ **Create a list** – Whenever you have a problem you need to tackle, you can get your creative juices flowing by creating a list. Let your creativity flow by listing as many solutions to the problem as you can.

- ♥ **Make focused and intentional changes in your life to boost creativity** – If you are static and perhaps in a rut, this can sometimes cause creativity blocks. So ensure you make regular changes to your daily life to keep creative channels flowing.

- ♥ **Work on the bad ideas** – You are being highly creative even if all you are coming up with are bad ideas; work on them and see if they can be developed in some way. You may find that it could end up becoming a solution to your problems.

- ♥ **Group Brainstorming** – A group of minds is more powerful than the one. Use groups to multiply creativity.

- ♥ **Always challenge others and yourself** – Challenge yourself by telling yourself that the same habits of the past cannot help you achieve different results going forward. This will force you to come up with new ideas and ways to find solutions to problems, which can generate some great creative ideas.

- ♥ **Tap into the logical part of the brain** – Your creativity lies within the right side of your brain. So give it a good nudge by activating the left side of your brain. Breathing in and out through the left nostril a few times can help.

♥ **Hire a divorce and life coach** – Working with a coach like myself can help if you believe your creativity is truly depleted or if you are stuck and overwhelmed, feeling unclear as to your creative ability. This can help you find your weaknesses, which makes it easier to correct and strengthen them.

♥ **Unleash your inner child** – think like a child – Go back to your childhood and let all your inhibitions as an adult go. Forget all the stress, worries and strains. There are no limits to a child's creativity, so when you feel stuck think like a kid and watch the creativity flow.

♥ **Relaxation** – If you are under intense stress, your energy can become depleted quite rapidly. Relaxation can help you recharge, clear your mind, and enable creativity to flow smoothly again.

♥ **Play brain puzzles** – Play brain puzzles and games regularly, this is one of my favourites and one I do personally. If you take your mind off a problem, and focus on a puzzle, you are stimulating the brain, which can lead to creative thinking.

♥ **Be intentional about creating positive new and fun memories together with your children** – Forming new memories together with your children will take them into the future with pride, happiness and confidence.

Guard your heart

It is important to always look at a relationship and ask your-self: 'what is it costing me to stay in this relationship?' In the event that you totally lose yourself in a marriage, your cost is excessive.

Sometimes a divorce can be a blessing in disguise in that it can force you to take a critical look at yourself and make the necessary changes to your life that your previous relationship had prevented you from making.

Chapter 10.
PEOPLE ARE KEY

"The most beautiful people we have known are those who have known defeat,
known suffering, known struggle, known loss, and have found their way out of the depths.
These persons have an appreciation, a sensitivity, and an understanding of life
that fills them with compassion, gentleness, and a deep loving concern.
Beautiful people do not just happen."

– Elisabeth Kübler-Ross

Divorce and separation, like bereavement, often takes quite a long time to come to terms with. You want to get used to being a proper new person and part of a couple no more, and this won't occur over night. People, usually, will expect you to get back to your old self once your divorce is sorted, but emotions do not fit tidily into legal procedures.

For many of us, it requires about one or two years before we start feeling ok again. Piece by piece, it will begin to get better. Kids will even need time to adjust.

Using outside help

There are numerous resources where you are able to acquire some assistance to get over the results of separation and divorce. Don't feel bad about requesting help. You can't always get it done by yourself. There is no shame in requesting help. A few of the resources you may turn to are:

♥ Friends

♥ Your GP, who might tell you about local places and experts who are able to help. This may include self-help counsellors and groups.

♥ A health visitor, should you still have young kids. Many health visitors really are a goldmine of helpful tips.

♥ Check your local library. They frequently keep details about local activities and groups.

♥ Counselling services. Yellow pages or your GP will be good places to begin looking.

♥ Local self-help groups. These may be for single parents, or separated or divorced adults. Gingerbread.org.uk has local groups from coast to coast for lone parents; there are also local Meetup groups which you may find useful. Visit www.meetup.com.

♥ Mediators and family lawyers, broadly speaking, will know about helpful local networks too.

Helping your children

Ending your marriage does not stop you being a parent. You are both going to remain parents for your whole lives. What you do, precisely, concerning the children matters.

It is helpful if you are able to tell the children together once both of you have agreed what you will say and which of the decisions you will discuss with them. However, even if this did not happen, it is not too late to implement a joint effort to help the children through this traumatic journey. As we all know and which I've have touched on earlier, children often believe that it is their fault. It is crucial that, where possible, both you and your 'wasband' do all you can to reassure your children that they are not to blame, and that both of you still love them greatly.

Attempt to keep domestic routines as normal as possible

It is tempting to try and make it up to the kids with extra treats; I did this by taking my daughters on luxury holidays abroad at least 3 times a year, but over time, you will find, just like I did, that over-compensating like this is not sustainable and that in the long run this is unlikely to help much. Extra hugs did and do go a long way however, and you may find they will become extremely clingy for some time.

You will need to inform their school. School work usually suffers because kids have other activities to concern them. It will help if their teachers realise why they might be having difficulty.

You should learn how to use a few of the skills that mediators and attorneys use. There are many publications that teach how to make use of negotiation skills and people skills that will help you articulate yourself better.

Apologising is extremely hard, but it is incredible how it often benefits a relationship. Clearly, it is excessively difficult when you are hurting inside to implement this, but it is usually worth taking the time, particularly when you have kids.

Chapter 11.

GIVING BACK

Let us now discuss some additional constructive coping strategies. Keeping yourself busy and engaging with other people in positive circumstances is an essential part of coping with divorce. If you allow yourself to dwell too much on the past, then your negative feelings about your ex will often be exacerbated and this will hinder your ability to function normally and move on with your life. Here are some suggestions to try:

Stay constructively engaged

Involve yourself in hobbies, work, travel or adult education. Occupy a brand new hobby that has forever interested you, such as a start-up business idea, a craft or learn how to play a guitar. These kinds of activities definitely assisted me in dealing with my break up because I found that they engaged my spirit and mind simultaneously.

Enjoy old friendships or make new ones

Life after divorce can present a golden opportunity to reacquaint yourself with old buddies – or meet fresh and interesting individuals with similar interests.

Speak with an expert Life Coach to really get your creative juices flowing

Surround yourself with coaches who are able to offer you physical and mental recommendations for dealing with divorce, such as a financial advisor, a masseuse and sometimes even your family's physician.

Implement a big change in scenery

Does everything in your house remind you how lonely you are? Then leave! Now may not be a great time to put your house on the market or up-sticks, but nothing ought to prevent you from getting away for an extended week-end. You can even consider rearranging furniture, changing wall hangings, getting a new duvet, or changing the drapery. Anything that makes your home different from what it was will help.

Just take that trip you have wished for and visit your loved ones or buddies who live away from town. Embark on a retreat alongside a religious or adult group. Getting out of the house you have lived in with your partner can offer a necessary change of perspective while dealing with divorce.

Find a support organisation

Support organisations are self-help gatherings attended by individuals experiencing the same types of circumstances. Broadly speaking, they are funded by community centres and religious bodies, some are even funded by the Big Lottery fund which gives grants to organisations here in the UK to help improve their communities. Wherever these support organisations are located their ethos is similar and will offer a face to face platform where those in various stages of adjusting to their divorce can get together to teach and support each other.

Online divorce support organisations are also available twenty-four hours per day on the web supplying a less personalised, but more reachable, support format. A word of caution however, regarding online support groups and networks is that many are infested by 'trolls' and cyber bullies – i.e. people who are there just to ridicule, bully and insult legitimate members. Make sure you keep a thick skin on and spontaneity handy when utilising online support networks.

Though there is absolutely no immediate 'cure' for the intense feelings that divorce triggers, there are several better and healthier ways to handle them in order to suffer less, and also to grow in self-compassion, strength and wisdom from having experienced it. Getting involved with other people and not hiding away from the world is definitely one of the most vital ways I have found of doing this.

The process of emotional healing begins with giving yourself the space to grieve and finishes with moving forward with your life. "No man or woman is an island" so don't fall into the trap of trying to do this, all of this, on your own.

Chapter 12.

FINDING THE BEAUTY IN THE WORLD AGAIN

"Being successful and fulfilling your life's purpose are not at all the same thing;
you can reach all your personal goals, become a raving success
by the world's standard and still miss your purpose in this life."

– Rick Warren

Reconnecting with your forgotten passions

When you were younger, long before marriage, you were probably passionate about a hundred things. Perhaps you loved a film so much that you had to watch it every single day. For me it was the film *Mary Poppins*. I wanted her to come and live in our house so she could teach me how to be magical and share love with many children all over the world. Or maybe you were fascinated with dinosaurs and sure you were going to become an archaeologist?

Growing up as a kid you either love something or you hate it. That's what it means to be passionate.

Then reality sets in; you grow up, get married, have 2.4 children and then get divorced and you realise you are lost; you don't know what to do with your life. If you are like most people, then chances are that while married, you probably would have found yourself subsumed into your marriage, supporting your husband and your kids and quite rightly so, but you kind of put yourself last. This ultimately meant that you ended up doing the things you love half-heartedly and not getting all that excited about anything or not doing the things you love at all.

Now the ugly face of divorce rears its head and you suddenly realise it is time to find you, who was once lost in married life, and reconnect to those old passions you once had. And find new ones, too.

The good news is that you alone, just like millions of people around the world, married, divorced or single you may have latent passions that need to be reignited or maybe you never fully came to grips with what your passions are. The even better news is that your divorce, can be channelled positively into an opportunity to discover your why or reignite your passions or both.

Here is some help to get you started:

Remember Your Old Goals

One of the best ways to find out what you are passionate about today is to think about what you used to be passionate about. When you were younger you probably wanted to be an astronaut or a princess or both and it's only as we get older that we are told to find something more 'adult' to be interested in.

However, just because we may have been inadvertently forced to bury those old interests and passions on account of marriage, and just because you or I might not realistically become an astronaut anytime soon, (although nothing is impossible in God – I feel a preaching coming on – ☺) that does not mean you or I cannot still chase a passion for space or for travel or for new horizons – whatever it was that originally drove us to feel so strongly.

Sit back, reflect and have a think about the things you lost touch with and why, then try to get back under the skin of those things to remember what it was about them that got you revved up.

Add a New Spin

Sometimes you will find, especially after getting married, that you lost interest in the things that once were so amazing to you and if that's the case then you shouldn't feel bad. There is nothing wrong with finding new things to be passionate about, especially now you are divorced. Remember, through the trauma, through the rain, the rainbow will appear ushering you into your new beginnings, so be intentional, be adventurous and discover these new passions or you could just as easily try adding a new spin to an old passion.

For instance, if you used to love drawing cartoons, maybe you could enjoy reading comic books all over again? I won't tell, if you don't; your secret is safe with me. ☺ If you were passionate about politics maybe you still are, but your views have changed; perhaps you could go back to school and take up a politics or get a law degree. If you are in the UK, perhaps you could try getting yourself on Question Time as a panellist.

Rediscovering old passions is about respect for the past but it's also about growth and development and not forcing a square peg back into an old, round hole.

Living in the moment

Another way to reignite your passions and a wonderful form of post-divorce recovery coaching is the art of learning how to live in the moment. The more you are able to do this, the more bliss you will experience. If you are always living for the future, you are never actually free to see the miracle of life, here and now.

If you are able to practice the following three things, your life will quickly transform significantly. You will start to make use of your inner child to live passionately and appropriately:

1. Practice Listening

One of the greatest blocks to recognising all life's extraordinary moments is that people usually don't stop to pay attention. We are not present, rather we are too busy speaking with ourselves. If we are thinking constantly, we are living entirely in an environment of symbols. We are residing in an environment of concepts about reality; phrases that label, categorise and describe things. This is often a great tool for communicating, but it is also a hindrance when it becomes unmanageable.

If we are always thinking, we are never in a relationship with reality. To be engaged with life, we've got to be present, pay attention and listen. Imagine that each time you interacted with somebody, you had been doing all the talking. There would be no communication since you never gave your partner an opportunity to speak. It works in the same manner when you are communicating with life.

Rather than thinking constantly and becoming lost in your ideas, decelerate and simply listen. Place your concentration on listening. Whenever you discover that you are wandering away in your mind, gently take your concentration back again to listening.

2. Practice Non-Judgement

Maybe you have realised that whenever you judge others, it instantly places you in an adverse or negative mood.

I have come to discover that, frequently, the judgements we make are because others aren't conforming to the way in which we would live. It is important to take on board that everyone's values will vary, and that is what makes life interesting. While there are several justifiable judgements you and I may make, they still may not be worth making, especially in our own Believe, Heal and Live Again post-divorce recovery reinvention journey.

Compassion is really a better vehicle for change than judgement.

Next time you are about to create a judgement, attempt the alternative; practice compassion. Even when it comes to you; when the tendency to be critical comes, please, please please show yourself a little kindness and practise self-compassion.

Let your feelings of having to judge be a reminder for you to practice compassion. This way, your negativity is going to be transformed into peace.

3. Open Your Heart

If you are similar to me and you are quite left brained, you may be wondering, 'Ok that is great, but how precisely do I open up my heart? '

Opening up your heart is really a matter of accepting yourself and life as it is. It is a matter of forgiving yourself and others. It is letting go of your resistance to the flow of life and the flow of circumstances.

If you wish to do things to alter something, that is fine. However it does not make any sense to resist what's already real. Surrender to this moment, accept things and people as they are, and your heart will start to open.

Ok, Zina – you have talked about how to rediscover old goals and reconnect with forgotten passions. What do I do when I don't know what my passion is? How can I find it?

How to find your Passion and Mission Statement when you don't know what it is

Imagine for a moment, you meet a person who is infectiously passionate about something. This is a person who truly believes in what they are doing; they eat, breathe and sleep it. Arguably, he or she could be the most passionate person you have met. Understandably, you might not necessarily share their passions, however, that doesn't mean that you can't appreciate their belief or their conviction. And in the vast majority of cases you probably will. People with genuine passion are magnetic, they're charismatic, they're infectious, and they're inspiring. In many instances, these become leaders in our communities, in our cities, in our countries and in our world, people who shape change.

"Zina, thank you for the rhetoric, That's all well and good, but what if I don't have an obvious passion? Ok, I get that, what if you are someone with 'passing interests' rather than passions? What if you are unable to sum up who you are or what you believe with a goal or a statement?

Knowing Your Mission

That there is huge power in knowing who you are and what you want cannot be over emphasised and, yes, this is what leads you to your passion. But that does not mean that you must be able to sum up your plan with a single statement in order to find what your mission in life is. No one ever said that your passion had to be a simple sound bite. The important thing is to learn how to listen to you, going through a self-evaluation questioning process by asking yourself the following key questions:

Finding your Passion self-evaluation questions

1. What do you do effortlessly and very well?

_____

_____

2. What are your key motivations?

_____

_____

3. What holds you back, are you afraid. If yes, why?

_____

_____

_____

4. Apart from your divorce or relationship, what do you consider as not currently working well in your life and career?

_____

_____

_____

5. What activities stress you out, makes you anxious or drains your energy so much so that you find it pointless and a waste of time?,

_____

_____

_____

6. What do you find engaging, fulfilling, enjoyable and consider as making a difference?

_____

_____

7. Who do you find most inspiring and motivational?

_____

_____

8. What makes your heart sing and excites you?

_____

_____

9. Are you living your authentic self or are you living a lie or a life of make believe?

_____

_____

10. Are you following your heart or following the crowd?

_____

_____

11. If money were no object how would you spend your time?

_____

_____

12. What are your core values and how does your current life support, align or reflect these values?

_____

_____

_____

13. What would you like your epitaph to be, what would you like to be remembered for?

_____

_____

_____

What I have found really interesting and intriguing is the fact that most of us have multiple interests and hobbies that we are passionate about, and more often than not there will often be an undercurrent running or common theme between them and in the main, that undercurrent will be partly inspired by our beliefs. Finding that undercurrent is the plan.

Mind Maps and Mood Boards

An excellent way to uncover these connections or the undercurrent in order to find your driving force is to create a mind-map or a mood board. In other words, write down and gather all the things that you find intriguing and fascinating or that you believe are important and put them in one place.

At the same time, write down the things you used to be interested in. What did you want to be when you were younger? And write down your role models and the people you look up to. Ask yourself, what do they have in common?

You can also try drawing pictures of what you imagine your perfect future to look like or of your happiest memories. Ok, you might not be a Leonardo Da Vinci and if this is the case, rather than drawing, how about cutting out pictures and images from magazines or printing off from things that resonate that you find online?

Once you do all this, take a step back and look at what you've created. What are the themes, the undercurrents that run through everything? What would your perfect world be like taking into account all these things? And what would you have to do to create that perfect world for yourself and/or for everyone else? What does good look like to you?

Right there is your mission and right there is who you are.

Chapter 13.
SO HOW DO I COPE?
COMPARTMENTALISING

Ok, I get it, you are saying, *"Zina, you want me to reawaken old passions, you want me to be less judgemental, you want me to live in the moment, you have even given me tips on how to find my passion when I am not too sure what or where it is.....aaah! Help! This thing called "from we to me" transformation is a lot to grapple with, so how do I cope?"*

For most of us, our tendency would be to allow our feelings to rule. We get so overwhelmed whilst in a hard situation like divorce, especially when we are relearning how to become a "me" all over again after first being a "we". I get that, having lived through this same journey. It is simple to get inundated, become overwhelmed, possess a narrow focus and lose perspective. *Compartmentalising* is definitely a necessary tool for coping with this.

The Titanic was initially pronounced as unsinkable' by her makers due to her numerous compartments. They said that, even if one compartment should flood, the boat would keep afloat simply because they would seal up all of the other compartments.

What they did not allow for was the iceberg piercing the areas of numerous compartments simultaneously, causing all of them to leak and the boat to sink.

Yes, I know you watched our dear Leo Di Caprio (before he became a hunk) and lovely Kate Winslet before the many divorces. I remember that tear jerker of a film like it was yesterday – I went to watch it alone – me and my bump – during the day at my local cinema. I had just gone past my due date with princess number one, almost 19 years ago. Most people came as a couple hugging one another, sharing the grief of the disaster as we watched it unfold before our very eyes on the screen. I remember a Chinese couple sitting about two rows in front of me, the man was inconsolable and kept sniffling while his partner took his head and cradled in in her arms. I rubbed my bump in circular movements over and over again as a deluge of tears flowed uncontrollably down my face.

Getting a little nostalgic there. Ok Zina, focus. The Titanic is a good example of what goes on when 'all the compartments get flooded', and the ship analogy is a good one to use when coping with divorce. Many writers have likened people to ships who are **on the ocean of life**.

So my question is how could you make use of the ship analogy to deal better with the downsides in your divorce so that you don't get so overwhelmed in your recovery?

Firstly, you need to ensure that all your other 'compartments' are kept 'tight and dry' and 'seal up' whichever compartment is 'flooding'.

Which means putting the problem in perspective and, very importantly, only considering it when it is directly before you and/or when you are taking action to solve it: "compartmentalisation".

A very unhealthy, though truly human and natural, tendency would be to become overwhelmed by a particular difficulty in your divorce and reflect upon it constantly. This is especially important throughout the time(s) when you can't change anything about it.

"Remember that compartmentalisation isn't denial or 'burying' the issue. It is just the opposite!"

While I was going through the issues in my marriage, it was incredibly tempting, especially while at the office, to brood about it and, a whole lot worse, to gripe to others about my domestic issues, I managed to keep a handle on that, only just, but what I did end up doing was to just stay at work right into the late hours because I couldn't face going home. And even when I got home, I would sit in my car for hours reflecting and lamenting.

But, there was a problem with that: I was at work, and there was nothing I could do about my domestic issues at that current moment. The only real issues I was able to solve and really should have solved at the office were my job issues within the core working hours. I actually could only resolve or attempt to resolve my domestic issues when I was at home and even at that only with the help of God and my wonderful support network.

The worst behaviour you are able to participate in is "brooding", "lamenting" or "reflecting" over an unhappy marriage or a consequent divorce situation. What is wrong with brooding? PLENTY!

To begin with:

♥ It magnifies the issue, which will be among the worst things you can do!

♥ It drains you of precious energy, energy that is needed to resolve the issue.

♥ It certainly makes you downright miserable!

So, let's delve deeper into what a practical, real-world use of compartmentalisation could look like. A good place to start is to just take the issue, put it in a 'water-proof' compartment and 'lock its doors' until:

♥ It's right before you, regardless of the reason.

♥ You are in a block of time you have deliberately set aside for focusing on it.

♥ You are ready and able, for whatever reasons, to do something positive about it.

Remember that compartmentalisation isn't denial or 'burying' the issue. It is just the opposite!

It's about keeping the issue 'contained' to ensure it does not 'spill over' into the remainder of your life, affecting every minute in an adverse way!

By compartmentalising, you will have more energy, more clarity, and much more mental stamina to focus on the divorce issues before you and solve them.

Chapter 14.

THERE IS A WINNER IN YOU; DON'T JUST LIVE - THRIVE!

 There's a Winner in YOU

Ann Gillian (1988)

It's only me
I've come to see you
And I know
What you have been through
I will be your friend
Lean on me for now
But to pull you back up
Somehow
I'll have no more of this moping around
I'm tired of you putting yourself down
But in spite of all you've been through
I still believe
There's a winner in you
Sometimes you can see it
From the tip of your mind
And can't focus at all times
If the wind touch you to another
Before you discover
There's a winner
There's a hero
There's a lover too
Somewhere
There's a winner in you
I'll have no more of this moping around

174

I'm tired of you putting yourself down
But in spite of all you've been through
I still believe
There's a winner in you
There's a winner
There's a hero
There's a lover too
Somewhere
There's a winner in you
There's a winner
There's a hero
There's a lover too
Somewhere
There's a winner in you

About 50% of marriages result in divorce, but those people facing it don't have to simply 'survive' to get through the experience. It is possible for there to be something more! Liken your divorce experience to a battle: you fight, you get a few bruises, maybe a bloody nose, but you thrive and emerge victorious because, if you really believe it, you will discover there is a winner in you.

I believe in you; that you are well able to aim for bigger things than simply surviving. You are reading this book because you want to learn how to thrive, win and reinvent yourself after divorce – especially if you are an individual who is divorced with children.

As a single parent myself, I cannot overemphasise that it is absolutely vital that you heal from your personal emotional pain so you can be a present, supportive and loving mum, going over and above the call of duty (this is a given), while at the same time making sure you shield the children from the possible cross-fire of separating adults. We always as adults like to say that children are resilient and yes they are to an extent but it is still our responsibility as parents to ensure they are as emotionally balanced as possible. In Chapter 20 – REFLECTION – I talk a lot more about single parenting and how to ensure your children's well-being is being taken care of.

Chapter 15.

IT'S OKAY TO BE SAD - BUT NOT FOR LONG!

"Recovering from divorce is like climbing a mountain,
one challenging step after another.
For most of us, it's a difficult journey –
but the rewards at the end of the climb are worth it!"

– Dr. Bruce Fisher and Dr. Robert Albert,
Rebuilding When Your Relationship Ends

As you embark upon the recovery process, you will definitely experience a dizzying selection of emotions. I know I certainly did. You might well spend time in a state of shock, not able to understand what is happening.

Like I said earlier in Chapter 2, I felt angrier than I had ever been before. I felt extremely betrayed and hurt and mourned the end of my marriage. I worried anxiously about my own future. I was ashamed and inwardly wondered what was wrong with me; why couldn't I sustain a simple marriage? You see for me, just like a lot of you, marriage is forever, just like in fairy tales and romantic movies – "…and they all lived happily ever after".

However, if you are mentally and emotionally healthy, you will ultimately start to heal and learn to accept what has happened and get on with your life.

Over time, (and I know it may not seem like it now) you will become available to new relationships, maybe even seeking them out. You will learn to cope with your ex-partner in a civil manner and, finally, you will remember the great times you and he experienced together. You know what? When I look back at my marriage now I am able to say to myself, if I had to do it all over again with the same man…I would. The hurt, pain and disillusionment was horrendous, but I look at my two wonderful and amazing daughters and say to myself…it was well worth it. Now, trust me, I didn't have these feelings overnight….but they will come to you too. Then you will be able to see something positive that came out of your broken relationship. It is at this stage that you will truly know that you are moving on and ready to Believe and Live Again.

If you discover you are unable (or unwilling) to come to terms with what has happened and move ahead with your life, you most likely should search for professional help. To be honest, I actually resisted seeking help initially when I was going through my own divorce. For some strange reason, at the time, which with hindsight was really a bad idea, I felt it would be perceived as an indicator of weakness.

Learning Point: Most people going through a traumatic experience like a divorce, will encounter periods of time in their lives where they could benefit from the help of a coach or a mentor or even a counsellor or therapist. I must emphasise that **it is not a sign of weakness**.

Don't Give Up On Hope!
Because there is Hope in your future.

In my experience, I have found that everyone needs at least a coach and /or mentor for any or all of the facets of their lives. It could be for business, career, relationships, sports and a whole host of other facets. Often times, we find ourselves feeling stuck in a rut and unable to move forward or achieve peak performance.

Divorce Recovery Coaching and/or Mentoring is extremely useful, be it in the area of your business, career, relationships, your health and wellbeing, before, during and after divorce, as well as any other area of your life. Divorce Recovery Coaching particularly is designed to help you identify and transform those areas of your life which you find unfulfilling or unsatisfactory before and especially after divorce.

Help will come in many forms, however, when it comes to mental health issues, this is a whole different ball game. Many people believe that contacting a counsellor, therapist or other mental health professional could lead to an extended amount of intensive therapy resulting in one becoming stigmatised. What you need to ask yourself is, if you have developed mental health issues as a result of the divorce or relationship breakdown, are you really ready to be healed or do you want to wallow and stay stagnant in your past?

The truth is, the stigma surrounding mental health is being reduced especially due to the awareness being raised by the media and by celebrities publically sharing their journeys, challenges and victories. A counsellor or psychologist might feel it is essential to see you for just a few sessions and does not judge your character. There might be a need to be sign posted to your GP for further diagnosis, referrals and treatment.

**The most important thing is to get help
and get it TODAY!**

If you are reading this and still feel uncomfortable with therapy or counselling, think about going to a support group or a Divorce Recovery Coach. Furthermore, many churches, synagogues and mosques, etc. provide such groups and services for individuals coping with changes like divorce. You will find organisations in your town listed online or in your local Yellow Pages.

You may also look for mental health services available in your town. If you do not want to go through your GP, many communities offer counselling services, sign posting along with other mental health resources at little to no cost, based on your ability to pay.

Keep the following considerations in mind if you are wrestling with the thought of searching for some help:

- ♥ Everybody experiences a period of time in life where they might take advantage of specialised help.

- ♥ There is no shame in seeking help for an emotional issue.

- ♥ Finding help can permit us to move forward, away from our issues, and get on with our lives.

- ♥ Taking the initiative to locate help is really a sign of strength and not weakness. It is a part of getting a grip on our lives.

If this is you, coping with depression for instance, staying in an extended depressed state is not necessary. Most medical practitioners and therapists recommend a mix of medication and counselling to deal with depression, anxiety, stress, panic attacks, and other ailments that arise as a result of divorce and it is frequently done successfully.

Change happens, so when it does, it is up to all of us to cope with it the very best way we are able to. Getting ourselves ready for change is really as simple as acknowledging that it will occur and having a support system in position for when it does.

Keep in mind that not all change is bad, but even good changes may cause stress. And if you discover you are having issues dealing with change, remember that there is help available.

Chapter 16.

THE REAL VALUE OF INTERESTS AND HOBBIES

After divorce, it often appears like the world has stopped for you personally. Instead of being ruled by this, it is best if you are able to be the master instead, because moving forward in life is really essential after divorce. Use this as an opportunity for learning what you need to learn, let go of the rest and move on – upwards and onwards; If we choose to, we are all able to learn from our experiences, negative or not.

Following the divorce, it is important as part of your emotional healing, recovery and reinvention process to search for new things to experience that will put that smile right back on your face. From my own experience, I have found that it is important that you begin to explore and adopt new hobbies, in the local community as well as in your house.

I found that after the tears comes the sun and when that period in your life emerges you will quickly discover that there are so many life changing and impactful activities that can occupy the hours. If you are a loner or an introvert, so be it. You may want to use your time acquiring new skills like attending art classes, joining a film club, making pottery and so on. You could do what I did and try your hand at writing, then become a writer! I have always written; as a child, I started writing by keeping a daily secret journal of my deepest thoughts, crushes, and plans for my future...which I must add included getting married to a handsome prince and living happily ever after ♥♥.

As I grew older, I graduated to writing short stories and articles based on my observations of the world around me and sometimes even included personal incidents. I also intertwined my present emotions as part of the plot.

Research has shown that one of the most enduring methods for surviving trauma of any kind is writing out feelings. Divorce certainly qualifies as "trauma," and journaling is a good way to help you get through the pain, anger and sadness many of us experience during such an event. I certainly found it extremely cathartic and continue to do so.

Today, what started as a hobby when I was a child has been instrumental to my own self-discovery, healing, recovery and amazing transformation after divorce. I still write profusely keeping journals and writing blogs, articles and short stories as well as providing expert comments and contributing to guides and reports all over the world. I have found my writing journey both therapeutic and very rewarding. This may be you too, but you will never find out if you do not try.

I appreciate that you might be saying, *"that is ok for you Zina, you have been graced with a natural flair for writing"* and therefore be among the thousands of women around the world who often say they aren't "writers" and believe they can't journal because they think they must be good writers.

One thing I would like to say here in response is that when journaling, you do not need to pay attention to spelling, punctuation, grammar, or creative phrasing because your journal is private and for your eyes only. The key objective of journaling is to pour out your feelings, deepest thoughts and musings without analysing them so writing becomes free-flowing and edit-free.

Writing may be a physical act, but when you put pen to paper and really let your mental editor go free flow, your feelings will appear and pour out without effort.

Here are some basic tips to get you started:
1. Forget about grammar, spelling and turn off phrases.
2. Write until you feel finished.
3. If you are new to journaling, start out with old-fashioned pen and paper. You can switch to your PC, laptop or iPad later.
4. Write in blank journals that are published precisely for this purpose.
5. Try not to edit as you write; but rather accept whatever comes up.
6. Use guided journaling in books such as *The Divorce Recovery Journal* by Linda C. Senn and Mary Stuart, M.A.

You may experience difficulty trying to figure out the difference between your thoughts and your feelings. Why don't you think back to the last time you were angry, for example. Think about your physical symptoms. What were they then? What are they now as you think back? Perhaps you find yourself feeling hot (raised blood pressure), or have a sudden rapid heart rate (rise in adrenaline), faster breathing, and perhaps other physical symptoms. These can all be the result of emotion.

Your feelings and emotions are located in the body. Thoughts, on the other hand, are abstract entities. If you're unsure whether you're thinking or feeling, take an inventory or an audit of how your body feels.

At the beginning, write whenever you feel the need. Eventually, feelings will begin to change and your journaling will evolve with them. When you first begin to journal your feelings about your divorce, please don't reread immediately. Wait at least two weeks or even longer before looking at what you've written. Allowing time to elapse enables you to see your own growth and progress.

Feelings are so temporal and fleeting that often we can't even recall how we felt about certain issues or people. Keeping a journal captures your own personal history. In addition to giving yourself an emotional outlet during a troubled time, you're also giving yourself a historical record that will allow further reflection at a later date.

For this book, I have had to go back to journal entries from years and years ago, and there are many entries I don't ever recall writing; the sheer feeling and emotions that jumped up out of the pages to me has been exhilarating; there have been some bitter sweet moments too as I recall incidents now. In some places, I look at entries and I say to myself, *"Zina did you really write that or go there or feel that?"* But all in all I have always found journaling therapeutic and calming, going down memory lane in written form has been no different.

Writing has always been one of my favourite hobbies. It might not be your thing but trust me, in your own journey, you will discover that lots of hobbies can grow to become a career option for you, letting you utilise your time and effort in a far more productive way.

Socialising and networking has become a hobby that many women enjoy and provides several choices. You could join a swimming club or bowling league. You could participate in a cake decorating class or a knitting circle. Dance lessons are a great way to get back to interacting with people. Join a jazz, ballroom or Zumba class.

Each one of these activities can not only cause you to become happy, but you will also have the ability to learn something new. You do not have to go alone. You could always take a good friend or close family member along with you to be your companion. This will all certainly be a good experience. If these things do not really suit you, then just try doing something which you are more familiar with and you will enjoy.

If you were very sporty in your youth, you could always train to become an assistant coach to your local community team; rather you than me, I might add. ☺ You could coach sports like Netball, Swimming, Basketball, Hockey, even Football or what our cousins stateside call Soccer. You may also want to get involved in charitable pursuits such as fund raising for your chosen charity or participating in charity events in your local church for instance. In my local church, I am a volunteer with a team who cook and serve a full English breakfast each Saturday morning to the homeless and marginalised within our local community. I have been doing this for over ten years and have found it extremely fulfilling and rewarding, especially as it has taught me the real meaning of gratitude and putting things into perspective. No matter what I have gone through, hearing our service users' stories each week, especially from the single parents amongst them, has made me realise I have a perfect life in comparison.

These are just a few of the services that you may decide to get involved with.

You have boundless opportunities before you, go ahead and look for anything that will capture your attention and hidden talents. This is ideal because all of the pain and sorrow will be quickly forgotten and you will be in a far more positive mind-set. If you are busy on all of your new hobbies, there is less chance that you will be bogged down by memories of the negative experiences that have happened. This will go a long way to minimising the potential of you falling prey to bad health-endangering habits. Instead, you will find yourself full of optimistic energy.

You could take classes at the local leisure centre, school or community centre. You could learn to cook, write, paint or do any activity that provides you with energy and causes stimulation. The secret is that you only have to find things that interest you. You may also develop hobbies based around the house. You could visit antiques fairs with a friend or even redecorate your whole house. Again, anything that will help to refocus attention to the plus points of your life will, undoubtedly, be great and will hasten your recovery process and help you discover a passion and purpose you did not even realise existed.

Chapter 17.
LOVE THOSE WHO LOVE YOU

Even if you took the tough decision of filing for divorce, it may be difficult both physically and mentally to be in the right mind set.

Your decision to file for a divorce (if this was you), and frequently the events prior to this decision, often still produce a feeling of loss. These feelings are much like those undergone when a family member dies. The truth is, a break up is a form of death. It is the death of promises made by somebody you used to love and hold dear, and it is the end of any future with this individual.

With divorce usually comes depression, so gathering all your family members around you for support is vital. Friends and family members are usually at a loss when divorce becomes an issue. This is not because they do not care. Often people just have no idea of what to say and do not know if they should say "well done" or "that is terrible", so frequently they do not say anything more. I found it better, sometimes, to bring up the divorce first to encourage them to help me out.

Let your family members understand what your emotional requirements are. If you are OK with the problem, inform them that your divorce is in your best interest. If you are experiencing sadness and stress, inform them that you will need their support emotionally. Good friends and family members will respond accordingly.

Do not allow anyone to be judgemental about you and make you experience guilt even if you initiated your divorce. Firmly, but kindly, let well-intentioned friends and family members realise that it has been for the best to finish your marriage. Unless other people have walked in your high heels and in your footsteps, they cannot completely comprehend your true emotions.

15th February 2012

Dear Journie,

Everywhere I turn I can see the remnants of Valentine's Day. The heart shaped chocolates on the shop shelves in Tesco, now marked as "reduced", I see significant others shuffling guiltily down the aisles looking for that bargain lingerie or perfume to appease their women, love is still in the air and it is beautiful. Then I ran into Ophelia, I tried to dodge but she caught me as I too was sorting through the valentine special lingerie for myself, I mean Whitney did say "learning to love yourself was the greatest love of all.

The truth is that well-intentioned family and friends can sometimes hinder your healing. Although it is often the case that you require support at the start, the time will arrive when you are able to stand up for yourself. Unfortunately, we may not realise this, especially because at times we are surrounded by friends and family who are still angry, depressed, bitter, vengeful or confused on our behalf.

Emotions and attitudes can be contagious. It is not possible to get on with your life when your mum is still wrapping you in cotton wool. It is hard to forget and forgive if your best friend keeps reminding you each day that your ex was a piece of garbage. How can you find compassion in your heart while your co-workers are baiting you to exact revenge?

Remember the old proverb regarding sleeping dogs? Yes it is best to let them lie. You understand the concept.

Remaining furious and compounding the negative parts of your relationship or divorce will not get you any nearer to being free. Instead, it will just ensure that you stay trapped within your pain. Indifference is the opposite of love. If you are hating, you are not progressing, you are not forgiving and letting go. And, should others be helping you to hate, they are also damaging your progress.

To achieve optimal mental vitality, be aware of the true feelings of the loved ones surrounding you. Concentrate on the here and now and get your friends to encourage you towards your fresh and better life. Learn from your past and then release it. Your future will definitely reward you for doing this.

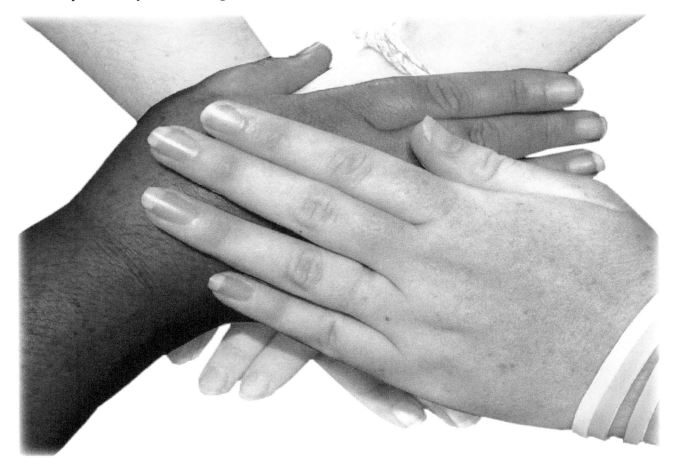

Chapter 18.

SPIRITUAL DETANGLING AND LEARNING TO LOVE YOU!

A spiritual divorce is one which we utilise to enhance our existence, thus the experience becomes positive instead of negative. A spiritual breakup connects us to our higher selves and bridges the division between our soul and our ego.

Whenever we use our break up to repair our wounds and grow as well as to learn and advance ourselves into becoming more conscious, loving people, we will have undergone a spiritual awakening and liberation of our souls.

Instead of remaining trapped in the trauma of our broken heart, a spiritual breakup allows us to re-establish the greatest facets of our existence. It is here, in the current presence of our highest self, our identity in God, that people can reclaim their joy, power and the unlimited freedom to produce the life-style of their dreams.

The pain of divorce stops your defences from working, leaving you in a position of complete vulnerability. It is only in this state of vulnerability that people become quiet enough to see the higher realities of peace and contentment.

You should realise that the breakdown of your relationship could be for a larger purpose. Understanding a few of the basic spiritual laws will help you discover that there is an explanation for why you are experiencing this pain.

The most crucial spiritual law is that everything is really as it ought to be. Nothing occurs accidentally and you will find no coincidences. We are always evolving, whether we know about it or not. Our lives are created so that we can obtain precisely what we need to support our very own, unique evolutionary process.

But most of us don't follow our instincts. When we stop fighting and submit to the problem just as it is, everything begins to alter. Resistance remains the major culprit in denying us our chance to heal. We resist out of the fear that, when we surrender, our lives will be out of control and we will be confronted with circumstances that we cannot handle.

Once we are prepared to examine our circumstances and confess that we do not understand how to repair them, we will be ready to obtain the assistance we are in need of.

- ♥ We can become accountable for and the designer of our very own new reality. We are able to split up from our partner by firmly reclaiming the facets of ourselves that we've projected onto them.

- ♥ We are able to distinguish what our self-defeating behaviours have been and learn to act rather than react in difficult situations.

To select a spiritual divorce would be to opt for your divorce in order to heal yourself. You can decide to work hard and heal yourself on the deepest level possible, or you can just be a victim of life, going along with other people's issues.

Quite simply, you can either control your divorce or you can let your divorce control you. Before you manage to locate and embrace the benefit of any situation or problem, it will continue to control you. It will hold you prisoner and you will carry it around like a gaping wound everywhere you go.

Be Conscious of your Self-Worth

Being conscious of your self-worth is all about you, not about your bank balance. I touched on this earlier. It's about the person you are in life. How often do we give to ourselves the respect, care, love and consideration we give others? Your self-esteem and self-care regime will be in direct correlation with how much you value yourself.

If you have a healthy self-esteem, some of the benefits you'll experience are:

♥ Happiness

♥ Independence

♥ Cooperation

♥ Ability to adapt to change smoothly

♥ Flexibility

♥ More positive outlook

However, an unhealthy self-esteem can cause:

- ♥ Unhappiness

- ♥ Fear of change

- ♥ Irrational thoughts

- ♥ Rigidity

- ♥ Defensiveness

- ♥ Negative outlook

- ♥ Paranoia

How you see yourself has much to do with how others see you. People want to be around you if you are happy, positive, smiling, and full of confidence. If we portray this and totally respect ourselves, others will start to respect us accordingly. After all, how can you expect others to respect you if you cannot even respect yourself?

Finding and developing your self-worth is heavily reliant on your self-esteem. So let's delve a little bit more into self-esteem and how you can develop it.

High Self-Esteem

There are many positive traits associated with a high self-esteem and self-worth. So it's imperative you develop these. Here are some of the traits you are likely to develop:

- ♥ Confidence in your abilities

- ♥ Knowing yourself and your identity

- ♥ Ability to display your true feelings to others

- ♥ Relationship will be free from intimacy problems

- ♥ Recognition of your own achievements

- ♥ Your ability to forgive others and yourself for mistake.

Low Self-Esteem

As mentioned earlier, low self-esteem is detrimental. Let us look into this issue a little further. Your thoughts will follow a certain pattern if you have issues with low self-esteem and low self-worth. You will be thrown off by the following traits:

- ♥ Insecurity and lack of belief in yourself
- ♥ Issues showing and accepting intimacy in relationships
- ♥ Struggling to show your true feelings
- ♥ Resistance to any form of change
- ♥ Inability to forgive yourself and others
- ♥ Struggle to recognise and give yourself true credit for your accomplishments

Develop Your Self-Worth

Following a divorce, there are a plethora of ways to build up your self-esteem and develop your self-worth so that you more equipped to have positive outlook about yourself and of your life in general, regardless of the circumstances that have tried to bring you down You may not believe this at the moment, but developing resilience and giving your self-worth a boost, even during the most traumatic periods of a divorce, is possible. Here are some tips in achieving this:

- ♥ Take the time to listen and learn from others, especially from those who may have experienced a relationship breakdown or some other form of adversity. You may experience criticism but try your best not to take it personally. But rather view it as an opportunity to encourage personal growth and continuous improvement.

- ♥ I cannot over emphasise the need to take pride in yourself and celebrate even the most minuscule of your accomplishments.

- ♥ Take time out for yourself daily. Try meditation. I meditate regularly on the words of God in the Bible; the thing is, look within and see your good points. Imagine turning your negatives into positives in life.

♥ Do something you enjoy each day. This can be anything, like a sport, reading, a bath, a long walk, relaxing in the sun. You choose.

♥ Even if you know you should not be doing it, never deprive yourself of something you enjoy.

♥ Repeat positive affirmations to drive out negative thoughts and feelings. Always talk positively to yourself.

Positive Self-Talk: The Benefits

In life, one of the biggest and most powerful forces we can utilise is ourselves. Our thoughts dictate how we feel, which will have a big effect on how we deal with life in general. When you control self-talk by transforming it from negative to positive, you will start to gain more control of all aspects of your life and make essential changes.

How you deal with life has a direct relationship to how much you will succeed in life. T. Harv Eker says, "How you do anything is how you do everything" Yes, divorce is traumatising and stressful, but there's no need to add to the stress by your thoughts and words. Having a positive mental attitude will lead to a successful divorce rather than one packed with negativity and problems. You are looking at life through a different lens if you have a positive mental attitude, no matter how little your focus is. You will start seeing the good in people, resulting in optimum success for yourself.

The quality of life you develop is based on how you think and feel on a consistent basis, so changing the way you think and feel can drastically change the way in which you view and deal with life.

Generally, if you look at life with a positive mental attitude, you are more likely to bounce back from problems you may encounter on the way. An optimistic person will look at problems for what they are – temporary set-backs which will be overcome smoothly. You can take full control of your thoughts and feelings when looking at life in this way, and have the ability to transmute negative to positive experiences by the change of perspective.

Since you can only have one thought at a time, and they are either positive of negative, staying on the positive side will keep you optimistic and happier and will give you the confidence to achieve your goals.

Using Positive Self-Talk Daily – Affirmations

In order to establish a habit of positive self-talk, "confessions" (if you happen to be a Christian) or affirmations should be performed each and every day. You have most probably developed a negative habit all those years as your marriage was crumbling. So this may take a little time to overcome. The Bible says in Proverbs 18:21:

**"Death and life are in the power of the tongue,
And those who love it will eat its fruit".**

Therefore, my advice is that you should aim to start repeating positive self-talk approximately 50 times during the day. You can achieve this by talking normal, quietly or out loud. If you make the effort to do this, the benefits you will gain are plentiful, such as:

- ♥ Confidence

- ♥ Overcoming difficult situations

- ♥ Quitting bad habits

- ♥ Bouncing back from divorce smoothly

- ♥ Recovering from illnesses quickly

- ♥ Confidence to make positive changes in your life

Some strong and popular phrases you can start off with include:

- ♥ *"I love the person I am"* – This is ideal to build self-confidence and gain respect for yourself.

- ♥ Similar statements to this can include, *"I am the best"* and *"I am a good person"*.

- ♥ ***"I have an interesting challenge facing me"*** – This is handy for when problems arise, or you are experiencing some sort of difficulty. Rather than thinking of the issue in a negative way, imagine it being a challenge to strengthen you.

- ♥ ***"I have many excellent qualities"*** – Divorce issues should not be given the power to take anything away from you as a person.

- ♥ ***"I can do this!"*** – If you have doubts about facing a particular issue or task, repeat this statement out loud.

- ♥ ***"I am fulfilled as a person"*** – If you want to encourage positive thoughts about yourself and the world, use this. This makes you consciously believe you are already satisfied, creating an abundance mentality.

- ♥ ***"I am full of health, energy and vitality"*** – If you are not feeling too well or you're recovering from an illness, repeat this statement to encourage good feelings about your health and wellbeing.

- ♥ ***Finally, develop an "I AM" consciousness*** – The major path to recovery is your faith. Put energy into whatever you believe in. For me it was and still is God and the church, but be it the church, mosque, temple, synagogue, or any other house of worship, your faith can carry you when you stumble and edify you when you're feeling strong. They are all there to help, so seek help if need be.

This recovery experience is only temporary; it will have an end and there will be a new beginning. Be willing to move on from the past, forgive yourself and your ex. If you want to gain spiritual strength, developing an "I AM" consciousness is important, realising the power within you. Then the "I CAN and I WILL" consciousness will come naturally to you, and you will become it. One of the greatest affirmations of power is "I CAN and I WILL", which is acknowledging and being conscious of God's spirit within you, which will manifest once realised.

Be conscious of the fact that God is within you. This is how you will gather strength at a time when it is needed most. You must do these things mentioned above even though they may not be as easy as they sound.

Chapter 19.
IT'S A NEW DAY, IT'S A NEW DAWN "ME"

 **Feeling**

Nina Simone (1959, 1965)

Birds flying high you know how I feel
Sun in the sky you know how I feel
Breeze driftin' on by you know how I feel

It's a new dawn
It's a new day
It's a new life
For me
And I'm feeling good

Fish in the sea you know how I feel
River running free you know how I feel
Blossom in the trees you know how I feel

It's a new dawn
It's a new day
It's a new life
For me
And I'm feeling good

Dragonfly out in the sun you know what I mean, don't you know
Butterflies all havin' fun you know what I mean
Sleep in peace when day is done
And this old world is a new world
And a bold world
For me

Stars when you shine you know how I feel
Scent of the pine you know how I feel

Oh freedom is mine
And you know how I feel

It's a new dawn
It's a new day
It's a new life
For me
And I'm feeling good

For most of this book, we have been talking about the characteristics, internal emotional conflicts and experiences you go through as a result of having been a "we" in a marriage that no longer exists.

To successfully transition or move from a "we" into a "me" it is important that you undergo transformative work to develop and maintain your new freedom; your post-divorce mindset.

The first area is in relation to your beliefs. As a result of your marriage and subsequent divorce there will be a number of limiting beliefs that need to be released so that you can truly move on into the Reinvented YOU! Any way we look at it our beliefs colour our perception of the world and our experiences. This means that beliefs are true only because you believe them to be. If your beliefs are not congruent with excelling in life and receiving abundance after divorce, separation or a break up, it is very unlikely you will ever live the life you deserve. When your results are falling short of your desires, your beliefs are the logical place to make a change. Be careful, because what you believe can become actual fact. Don't let your limiting beliefs become your reality!

Many of the beliefs we hold most strongly are inaccurate. In addition, most of our fundamental beliefs are formed at a young age. We learn these beliefs through our experience or simply by having our parents or other authority figures 'tell' us what to believe. It's therefore very easy to see why we have beliefs that hold us back from experiencing all the abundance that God has ordained and we deserve. To become the new Reinvented YOU, it is important that you change your belief system and begin to embark upon ventures you are passionate about and believe in.

Exercise 10. Eliminating Limiting Beliefs

Choose a negative belief and begin the process of elimination:

Challenge the belief.

Suppose you held the belief that the rich get richer and the poor get poorer. Where did the belief originate? What was the source? Did you read it or experience it first-hand? Was it something you learned from a parent, teacher, or peer?

- Is the source reliable?
- Has this source been wrong about other things in the past?
- Is this person an expert regarding the belief?
- Do you have proof that your belief is accurate?
- Could the opposite be true?
- What if your belief is wrong? What would change?

_____

_____

_____

_____

How has this belief limited or harmed you in the past?

List all the times this belief has steered you in the wrong direction or stopped you from taking action. Visualise your past and re-experience the pain and disappointment this belief has created. Realise that releasing this belief is a positive and necessary step.

Create a new belief that serves you.

It's not enough to let go of a belief. *It's important to replace it with a new perspective.* What is a more useful alternative to your current belief? You might choose the belief that "anyone can attract wealth and abundance".

Make a list of alternative beliefs.

Choose the one that feels the most empowering.

_____

_____

_____

_____

Search for evidence that your new belief is possible.

Do you know any people who have remarried? Seek out examples of successful remarriages.

_____

_____

_____

_____

Have there been instances in the past when you've proven your new, desirable belief correct?

Make a list of all the times you've been successful in congruence with your new belief.

_____

_____

_____

_____

Get excited.

Visualise yourself living your new belief. How would your life change? How would that make you feel? Write it down. What would you accomplish? Write it down. Stick with this process until you feel a high level of excitement and enthusiasm.

_____

_____

_____

_____

Reinforce the new belief.

Repeat your new belief to yourself 100 times each day. This will only take a few minutes. Make time in the morning and evening to complete this task.

Beliefs are most easily formed through strong emotional reactions and repetition.
The previous step provided the emotion. This step provides the repetition.

Continue until your new belief is rock solid.

It's easy to slip back into old patterns of thinking. Continue the process of visualizing your new belief in action and performing the 100 repetitions until your new belief is unshakeable.

Your beliefs shape your results and your future. If you're dissatisfied with your post-divorce life, begin by addressing your limiting beliefs. New beliefs are easy to install. Consider how easy it was to install your previously held beliefs without intention. The key is to find evidence for the new belief, surround the new belief with enthusiasm, and remind yourself daily.

Chapter 20.

REFLECTION

As we draw to the close of our REINVENT YOU! Journey, all through this book, I have shared my thoughts, tips, anecdotes, and research centred on the theme post-divorce recovery and reinvention. Now for the last lap, let's bring it all together focusing on my favourite bits and bobs, as I reflect upon the six main areas that are close to my heart and my reality.

- ♥ Reinvention as a Single Parent
- ♥ Recovery and Reinvention after Domestic Abuse
- ♥ Career Reinvention
- ♥ Healing, Restoration and Reinvention as a Woman of Faith
- ♥ Reinvention, Dating and Remarriage
- ♥ Forgiveness

It is my hope that as you go through these areas you will find something that resonates, perhaps a word, a sentence, a paragraph or group of paragraphs or a whole section that you can grasp with both hands and use as a spring board to soar up high into your powerful believe and live again life.

Reinvention as a Single Parent

Ok, Zina what is reinvention as a single parent?

Now that you are a single parent, reinvention itself could be a change, a shift perhaps in style so much that your parenting appears to be entirely new and refreshing, creating a supportive, enabling, loving and reassuring environment for your children and of course for you. That is not to say you were not a good parent before the divorce, but now your child has only you, especially if you are the custodial parent, it is important that you rethink and remodel yourself to fit into this new unchartered role.

I am a single parent and I know first-hand that it can be a huge challenge not just financially but emotionally too. Nothing really prepares you for this new role especially if you become a single parent not by personal choice but by virtue of a divorce or relationship breakdown after living together for a significant length of time as man and wife or through the death of a spouse.

Who is a single parent? A single parent is a person who takes on the role of parenting children and maintaining the nuclear family by themselves as a result of death, divorce, separation, or personal choice.

This type of parenting is still a bit of a taboo in our society today although it has been around since the Second World War and has been on the up rise ever since. In fact since the 1980s the number of single parent families in the UK, in Canada and in the US has practically doubled. It is fair to say that single parenting has somewhat redefined the traditional nucleus of two parents and children who are living in the same house.

Whatever way you cut it, single parenting for whatever reason does have a significant effect on a family's way of life and, as I have found, requires major adjustments to the entire family emotionally.

I would be lying if I told you that being a single parent has always been plain sailing, because it hasn't, sometimes I got overwhelmed, stressed, exhausted, confused, frazzled and downright drained emotionally, mentally, physically and spiritually with the sheer magnitude of responsibility in terms of raising well adjusted, focused and beautiful young women, however rather than tell you how I felt, here's a wonderful prayer which captures a lot of the various emotions I went through daily as a single mother but more importantly I believe a lot of single mothers all over the world will be able to identify with too. I discovered this all encapsulating prayer during my research for this book. I have reproduced the prayer here with permission from the author, Dr Emmett Diggs, a retired ordained minister with a doctorate in psychology and personality development He currently serves as a pastoral counsellor and bible teacher.

Divorced Mother's Morning Prayer
By Emmett Diggs – April 10, 2013

Lord, it's morning now and it has come too soon. I'm so tired. Too tired to face another day or another responsibility. But there are two children in bed who need my help to get ready for school. Yes, I know they are my responsibility.

Jesus, when I got married I never dreamed that our love would die...that divorce was possible. But he is gone and I'm a single parent with this awesome task of rearing two children. It overwhelms me some days, and today is one of those days. I need Your help!

There is so much going on in their lives, and I've got to get up and face the music. Music? Yes to the tune of cooking breakfast, choosing clothes for them to wear, and then taking them to school. Honestly Lord, by that time, I'll feel like I've already done a day's work. But then I have to go to work. Fatigued, frazzled, and worn down describes me. Lord, please help me keep up.

Want to hear more, Jesus? Okay, here goes. Everything falls on me. After work, I'll rush to pick the children up; then take one to soccer practice and the other to a tennis clinic. When will it ever end? I'm struggling to keep it all together. The loose ends torment me daily! It's homework tonight and then bath time comes.

If only my kids would consider what I do for them every day. Please Lord, let them just show a moment of appreciation, just once. They don't and won't. They're so self-absorbed and into their world only. They just do not ever consider me… how tough all this is for me.

The Bible says somewhere, friends tell me, that you are my Friend. Please be my Friend first. There I go, sounding like my children. Me first… always me first. How did I get into such a mess?

What's that Lord? I'll be stronger for having been a caring, sacrificial mother. All things work out good for those who trust the Lord. Yes, I've been told that and that's why I'm turning to You this morning! I'm trying to put my life in Your hands, but tomorrow is my day to sit in the courtroom. I'm praying for a final divorce settlement, and then maybe I can move on. This has been lingering over my head forever.

Dear Jesus, I'll really need for You to be there; to sit beside me. I've never faced a divorce settlement… the coldness of a courtroom… the finality of that which I thought would never die. Please Lord, come sit with me.

But that's tomorrow. Right now I've got to go pick up the kids from soccer and tennis, head home to help them with their homework and then fix them something to eat. They'll be starving by then.

Oh my Lord, the sun's peeking out through those dark clouds! It's as if You're saying, "I have heard your cry my child." I can feel Your presence beside me right

now! I know You'll be with me tomorrow too. What was that Lord? We can do this together just as the sun broke through those dark clouds overhead. Wow. We can do this together. My confidence is up, Jesus, way up!

What did You just say, Jesus? Okay, I'll take it one day at a time. My Friend Jesus, did I hear You right? You are telling me that it won't be too long before my children will begin to appreciate me. Jesus, look at that sun now, it's so bright. I can almost hear my child saying, "Mom, how can I help?" Golly is that sun shining and forming a new day for me.

"Now child of Mine and mother of yours, just relax. You're in a constant rush. Demands may be everywhere, but they are wonderful children, just as you are my wonderful child!

"Now, be confident in your mothering, see the Son in the brightness of the sun, and believe in My plan for you and your children. Give Me your hand and we'll travel this parenting road together…hand in hand." The sun's out! Amen

Scriptures to Declare and Claim for yourself during these times:

Matthew 11:28 "Come to me, all you who are weary and burdened, and I will give you rest." (NIV)

John 15:15: "Instead I have called you friends." NIV

Romans 8:28: "And we know that in all things God works for the good of those who love him, who have been called according to his purpose." NIV

Matthew 28:20: "And surely I am with you always, to the very end of the age." NIV

Deuteronomy 4:7: "…the Lord our God is near us whenever we pray to him." NIV

Matthew 6:34: "Therefore do not worry about tomorrow, for tomorrow will worry about itself." NIV

If this is you or some or all of this prayer resonates with you, please be encouraged and know that feelings of resentment, guilt and despair are typical for the spouse who is left behind.

Grief is the most common feeling among spouses who are the person left behind and we have dealt with this exhaustedly in Chapter 2 when we talked about the stages of grief: denial, anger, bargaining, depression and acceptance.

The acceptance stage, especially when it comes to **navigating the parental landscape as a single parent, is tricky enough**. In addition, studies have shown that the children of divorce also have issues with acceptance. Many children feel left behind, betrayed, taken advantage of, unloved, at fault, and inadequate as a result of parent separations. If you do have children and you are now a single parent, I get the feelings of despair, anguish and sometimes sadness, but guess what? Your children are most likely going through similar feelings or worse and it is our duty as parents, single or not, to support them through this unwanted transition as best as we can. The interest of your children is of paramount importance. Our children need to feel loved, heard, encouraged.

I wish I could say that once the marriage is over the healing begins, but it is very often not the case and it is crucial that as a single parent you understand that unresolved issues with your ex-spouse have significant impact on your children too. This becomes very evident in the area of resolving co-parent conflict.

In 2012, Joanie Winberg, founder and CEO of the National Association of Divorce for Women and Children (NADWC) in America, asked parents the pertinent question, "Are you aware that your children see, hear and feel the anger and tension between you and your ex-spouse a lot more than you realise?" Winberg continued by listing the potential key shortcomings of children in divorce situations as being:

1. They are twice as likely to drop out of school as those from intact homes.
2. They are three times as apt to have a baby out of wedlock.
3. They are five times more likely to be in poverty.
4. They are twelve times more likely to be incarcerated; i.e. go to prison.

(McManus: Ethics & Religion Sept. 12, 2004 Column #1,203)

These are very disturbing statistics which as parents, no matter what country we reside in, we cannot afford to ignore on account of our own feelings of sadness, anger, resentment or the 1001 other feelings that contribute to our emotional angst I repeat: the interest of the children is of paramount importance in all this. They did not ask to be born.

On this premise, it seems to me that the acceptance stage is of utmost importance. For instance:

Accepting responsibilities – becoming a single parent means maximizing all your resources to take care of the family.

This means looking for all possible, even creative, solutions to solve a problem. You may be playing the blame game with your ex-spouse or partner, but this a negative luxury you cannot afford Blaming others for what happened is unproductive Instead, look for ways to address the problem.

A good example is looking for alternative ways to find transportation for your child's first day of school. Instead of screaming and whining that the absent parent is not pulling his weight, an alternative could be to try looking for relatives who can drop off the child or working around the parent's schedule to drop off the child to school.

Sadly the stigma and the statistics don't look too good for us single parents. But you don't have to be a statistic. Successful single parent families have made their family the top priority. This means determining non-negotiables and balancing commitments.

Here are a few tips I believe you will find extremely valuable especially as a divorced single parent or co-parent.

1. Tell your children the truth, with simple explanations. Tell them where the other parent is.

2. Try your utmost, and I know this may be difficult, to refrain from bringing up grievances or speaking derogatorily about the other parent to or in front of your children.

3. Don't discuss financial, legal or other disputes with your children. If you can do it and not discuss these issues, trust me, you will save a lot of unnecessary angst for your children as they grow up, especially your older or oldest child who may have had to assume a more adult responsibility as a direct result of the divorce. I once had a client whose 14 year old son spent a lot of his time doing online job searching and online Forex trading so as to help his mum in paying the household bills rather than do his school homework.

4. Avoid saying anything, which might discourage your children from spending time with the other parent and from pressuring them to take sides.

5. Constantly reassure them that they will be taken care of and be safe and secure; even though your marital love may have ended, parental love endures. It is probably a good idea to find out what your child's love language is. A wonderful resource to use is the book *The 5 Love Languages of Children* by Gary Chapman and Ross Campbell MD. According to the authors, The 5 Love Languages of Children are:
   a. Physical touch
   b. Words of affirmation
   c. Quality time
   d. Gifts
   e. Acts of service

If you reflect carefully you will soon discover that one of these five is your child's main love language. It is useful to identify so you are able to relate with your child on a deeper level and know whether what you are doing at any given time is filling up their "love tanks" or not. Apart from the main love language your child can also have a secondary love language and it is important that you identify what it is too.

> **"Nearly all parents deeply love their children,**
> **yet not all children feel unconditional love and care".**

I cannot stop singing praises for this book and over emphasise how much of an invaluable resource and parenting tool this book and the online assessments are. I still use mine today, having graduated to The Five Love Languages of Teenagers by the same authors. What you will find, and I have experienced this too, is that you grow as a parent with each stage or milestone your child reaches. For instance, now my daughters are teenagers, very opinionated ones at that, and I have come to discover that my daughters are bilingual when it comes to their love language.

One love language may slightly tip the others, but both my children have a second language that is almost as strong. Here's the thing, if you don't speak that language at the given time your child needs to hear it, your child will not feel loved, no matter how much love you show them in other ways.

Say for instance you discover that your child's love language is **Physical Touch**, perhaps they:

- ♥ love to get and give regular spontaneous hugs, kisses;

- ♥ also love physical activities, like hugging, tickling, play fighting, dancing competitions, tag, climbing into your lap or even into your bed….yes! even as teenagers... (no princesses named here ☺).

Some quick wins for you as a mum could be to have loads of family cuddles, holding hands, snuggling up together on the couch, telling stories, telling jokes, sharing funny recaps from each of your days at work or school, perhaps playing games like ISpy or hand clapping games.

Or perhaps your child's love language is **Words of Affirmation** because they enjoy being told by others that they have done a wonderful job. They also enjoy giving recognition to the good efforts of others. If this is your child, their favourite words could include:

- ♥ Wow! You did that?
- ♥ Amazing
- ♥ That is really great
- ♥ Good girl, good boy
- ♥ Oh My Days – Fantastic
- ♥ Great job!
- ♥ Well done!
- ♥ I am so proud of you
- ♥ I love you

Write notes on the bathroom mirror, give compliments. Be sure to speak positively about your children, tell them always that you love them by saying "I Love You", Praise them aloud around others, Write a letter to them; in all you do be specific in your praise.

If your child's love language is **Quality time** you may find that they love to do things with you, perhaps to:

- ♥ go to the cinema and watch a movie, or stay at home and organise a weekly, duvet clad family favourite TV show;
- ♥ go out to eat, shopping, run errands, play a game, road trips.

If this is your child or children, you may notice that they also try their utmost to have your undivided attention, this could present by them wanting to sit close to you or have you watching them in the background while they are playing, doing homework or even online shopping.

Your child's love language may be identified as **Gifts**. Such children love it when they receive gifts or a special present or surprise. These children not only love receiving gifts but love seeking out wonderful gift ideas and thereby giving thoughtful gifts and presents.

If this is your child, you will notice the glee and happiness that lights up their face upon receiving a present or gift or special treat or having something special done for them. A good quick win would be for you to leave gifts for your child or children when you're out of town or perhaps go shopping with them for that special gift.

Last but not least is **Acts of Service**. Children with this love language like it when people do nice things for them, like helping with their uniform washing, helping with other household chores, driving to and from places. These children are also incredibly thoughtful and love helping others. Encourage your child by going on errands together like shopping, dry cleaning, interior design; eat together, plan holidays, special trips and events together making sure you are paying attention to every detail.

6. If you have more than one child, another tip is to spend as much time as possible with each child individually. From experience this one is a challenging one, but you will soon see the need if you haven't already. Each child will often use ploys to get your sole attention and may even guilt you into thinking you love one child more than another. As a single parent, sharing your love and attention equally and fairly is indeed challenging especially when it comes to settling sibling rivalry and conflict. "It's not fair" and "You love him more than you love me" or "How come when Julie did it you didn't say anything?" Communication is the key to an open relationship. Clear communication channels foster an open relationship between you the parent and the child(ren). I hear it gets easy as they grow into adulthood – I am almost there – phew!

7. Establish routine – Routines before the divorce or death should be kept because this is the child's only anchor showing that things have not drastically changed. Walks on the park, reading bed time stories or the usual Christmas dinner should be continued even after the death or divorce.

8. On the presumption that you are on civil speaking terms with your ex-spouse, keep agreements you make with him/her and be reliable and prompt, enabling the children to feel they can depend on and trust both parents. Avoid scheduling activities for the children which may conflict with the visitation schedule and, if unable to keep the scheduled arrangements, notify the other parent as soon as possible. If you are not on speaking terms, this becomes trickier to navigate. From experience as the custodial parent for my two teenaged daughters, what I have done is to empower and give them more control to manage their own schedules thereby encouraging a more independent relationship with their father. Interestingly enough, I have watched from the sidelines how they have successfully built up boundaries around their time and schedules, firmly communicating their availability for planned outings. In any event, whatever the case may be, the learning point here is that as a parent (whether you or your ex-spouse) it is crucial to establish open and clear communication channels between you and your children and to understand what their wants and needs are and how best to fulfil these wants and needs.

9. Do not, I repeat, do not use your children to get back at or send messages to your ex-spouse. Children in the crossfire get terribly wounded. In addition, try your utmost to avoid arguments, fights and threats in the presence of your children, no matter how old they may be, as the memories will be with them for a long time to come and could frighten and damage them, affecting their abilities to form their own healthy, well balanced relationships when they grow up.

10. Children often feel responsible for the divorce or may try to bring parents back together. Let them know they are not to blame and that the decision is final.

11. It is a well-documented fact that divorcing parents may feel guilty and overindulgent. My advice would be to set limits and boundaries with your children. This is something I wish I had done a bit more, especially with regards to shopping sprees and holidays around the world. Well, you win some and lose some. ☺

12. Continue to be the parent and seek other adults to fill your relationship needs. Don't allow your child to become "man of the house" or "little mother". This advice is pivotal to helping your children grow into well-adjusted responsible adults.

13. Where it is prudent to do so, arrange for both parents to be notified and be authorised to act in an emergency. Keep the other parent, school and nursery advised of your current residence address and telephone numbers.

14. One thing is for sure; you will continue to be parents throughout your life. Make an intentional effort to set aside your personal feelings towards each other and try your utmost to maintain an attitude of tolerance, decorum and flexibility.

15. Last but not least, taking care of YOU is key. You cannot give what you don't have – you cannot give of yourself if you don't replenish yourself. As a parent, especially as a single mother, if you do not take control of your life, taking control of child(ren)'s life becomes difficult. Self – care and self-compassion must be your watch word or mantra, but more than that you must commit to doing this. Be deliberate and intentional in your self-care regime emotionally, physically, mentally and of course spiritually. Taking care of yourself is not only good for you in terms of your recovery and reinvention but it also in terms of building the resilience you need as a parent so as to ensure a positive environment of hope and love is present in the family. To achieve this, patience is key – be patient with yourself and your children. This is an incredibly difficult time and you are entitled to reach out for help and support.

This was an important lesson I learnt in my journey. I used to get anxious, sleepless nights, stressed, and simply overwhelmed with the sheer enormity of being a single mother. I wanted to be perfect, not to let my daughters down and guess what? I was running and letting myself down. I learnt the hard way that if you are running on empty or if you even end up dead you cannot give what you don't have, which does include your life too.

There is a three year gap between the ages of my daughters and when the first daughter passed her 11 Plus exams and got offered a prestigious place into our local grammar school which places a lot of emphasis on cultural experiences for their students, my daughter and I were ecstatic.

However, as the custodial parent, it was not too long before I got acquainted with the regular school trips abroad, after school sports and extracurricular clubs and private lessons that **I had to pay for** on top of uniforms that needed perpetual replacing (both my daughters are very tall – "nuff" said!). Three years later, when my youngest daughter followed in her older sister's footsteps, and got admitted into the same grammar school, suddenly here I was paying all over again for the regular school trips and cultural exchange programmes abroad as well as the other school-related financial commitments. I truly believe, that at the time, I was drowning. After bearing my heart to God, I would psyche myself up and roar in the mirror *"Zina, with God on your side, you've got this!"* My first daughter is now in University, so I guess that is a victory roar I will be making for some time to come as my second daughter will also be attending University in three years' time too.

Notice, that I have written "I had to pay" in bold. Some of you reading this might undoubtedly say to me, "Zina, it's a choice to pay for these expenses". Yes I did have a choice; the choice I made was to refuse to let my children feel penalised because their father walked out on us. It has taken (and still does) resilience, audacious faith, admittedly some sleepless nights of worry, and doing the sums and relentless drive to ensure they have all they need to excel in their world and soar from where I left off.

I'm sure a lot of you can relate to this. It's hard to say "no" to your children, especially when they're not really asking for unreasonable things that they need.

Although as the custodial parent, I get far too much of the bills, tears and tantrums, I also get the smiles, the laughter, the hugs, the fun memories and, most importantly, genuine quality time with my girls; that's worth far more than rubies.

Co-Parenting

Are you a co parent? Here are some valuable strategies to help you minimise the incidences of parental conflict:

1. Leave your ego at the door and let go of any animosity towards your ex-spouse – love your children much more than any feeling you have towards your ex, whether positive or negative!

2. Even if you only communicate via email or text, make sure to always be polite; say please and thank-you. You don't need to like your ex but you should respect them and treat them cordially.

3. If both of you as parents get stuck and cannot work through an issue; consider receiving help from a mediator

"Co-parenting with your ex is a partnership – don't turn it into a competition."

4. Make every joint decision in the best interests of your child/children

5. Maintain good boundaries – if your children have an issue with the other parent, don't take it as an opportunity to begin bad mouthing him/her to them. Encourage them to direct their frustration back to the other parent so that they are equipped to resolve the issue maturely.

6. You and your ex-spouse will not always or may never agree on issues concerning your children. Own that fact, get on with it and pick your battles wisely, keeping the discussion amicable where this is at all possible. Let go of any pet peeves you may have had during the marriage or have developed now after the marriage.

7. There may be times where you have to go it alone financially. Have some savings in place or set aside a little every month that you can use towards treats for your children or to solve a school or parenting responsibility. Having said that, it's also very important to find some way to compromise with your children, communicate boundaries that you may not always give them what they want, but that doesn't reflect at all on your abilities as a parent.

> *"Fear not, for I am with you;*
> *Be not dismayed, for I am your God,*
> *I will strengthen you,*
> *Yes, I will help you,*
> *I will uphold you with My righteous right hand"*
>
> **– Isaiah 41:10 NKJV**

Apart from standing on the Word of God, as a single parent with almost sole emotional and financial responsibility for the upbringing of our daughters, what has helped me a great deal in times of resentment has been seeing my relationship with my ex-spouse as being completely new – outside of him and I Our relationship is purely about the well-being of our children. Our marriage is over, but like it or not we're still a family and, for me anyway, my daughters are my top priority.

The last point I want to leave with you, is that forgiveness is everything. I recognise it can be difficult to forgive your ex-spouse or even forgive yourself after the breakdown of your marriage or relationship, however I guarantee you, if you are able to do this one thing, it is truly a wonderful legacy to leave your children when God decides it's your time to come home. Co-parenting is not about your feelings or those of your ex-spouse, but rather about your child's happiness, stability, and future well-being. Really, what's more important than that?

Recovery and Reinvention After Domestic Abuse

Abusers are typically very manipulative and often manage to convince you that you are weak and worthless. I have a message for you – it is not true. YOU are neither weak nor worthless; your worth is more than rubies. Perhaps, having been told this over and over again, you will need the strength to move on to change your mindset and I know it may be hard to believe, but there is a silver lining after abuse.

We all know the story of the living rock icon Tina Turner who survived an extremely violent relationship with Ike Turner. She suffered his violent attacks on an almost daily basis and in 1976, 14 years after they were married, she finally escaped after he'd beat her bloody by waiting until he slept, sneaking out and never looking back. Tina realised that having the courage to leave this life-ruining relationship made her a much stronger woman and she continues to inspire other abused women to take a leap of faith and free themselves from their violent partners. Today, she is a phenomenal, iconic ageless woman who has lived a hugely successful and happy life after leaving Ike Turner. Tina is true living testimony that you can recover and reinvent yourself after abuse.

Domestic violence and abuse is all about power and control so please don't blame yourself for allowing it to happen. You are not alone. It is a well-established fact that both physical and sexual abuse and threats to commit them are the most apparent forms of domestic violence. The positive thing is that these are typically the very actions that help raise alarm bells enabling others to become aware of the situation. However, regular use of other of forms abusive behaviours by the perpetrator, when reinforced by one or more acts of physical violence, make up a larger system of abuse. So even if you were in a marriage where physical abuse occurred only occasionally, this is sufficient to instil fear and the threat of future violent attacks. This in turn is often what allowed your ex-spouse or partner to take control of your life and circumstances.

The Power and Control diagram below is a particularly helpful tool to help you understand the overall pattern of abusive and violent behaviours, which may have been used by your ex-spouse to establish and maintain control over you. This leads to a firmly established pattern of intimidation and control in the relationship.

But that was then here is now!

I have to say for even reading this, you are no longer a victim. It is immaterial who filed for the divorce; if your marriage was an abusive one, those shackles have been broken and your spirit, your very essence as a woman has been released and freed. Freed to become the woman you were meant to be, a reinvented strong woman of purpose, passion and poise. How?

- ♥ **By forgiving yourself** and accepting that you are loveable

- ♥ **Accept that you deserve respect**

- ♥ **By severing all contact after divorce; don't engage.** If you have children, agree/arrange visitation via Social Services contact centres. Your ex may attempt to contact you after your relationship has ended. The first step is to make this harder for him by not leaving any path to follow. Move home, change telephone numbers and email, close down your social media channels, and warn all friends and families to not reveal any information. Do everything possible to prevent contact and if he does try to get in touch – DO NOT RESPOND! Ignore emails, calls and texts. No matter how sincere or apologetic your ex may seem, they are still trying to manipulate you and control you. To begin to move on, recover and reinvent, you must be utterly free from them.

- ♥ **By understanding that you are not to blame.** If you were buried deep in an abusive marriage or long term relationship for a long time, it is understandable if you felt at the time like something must be wrong with you, otherwise why would your husband or partner choose to treat you so badly? Please, please please! You must begin by reaffirming yourself and acknowledging that it is NOT you. This is the first step toward rebuilding your self-esteem after being released from an abusive marriage and ending up divorced.

- ♥ **By seeking support and help.** Talk to trusted friends and family. Don't isolate yourself from the people who care about you. Being alone solves nothing and it is exactly what your ex wanted; to cut you off from any support. Reach out to close family and friends. Explain to them what has been happening and show them any evidence (like photographs) that you might have. Surround yourself with people who are supporting and caring as these are the people who will help you through this difficult time in your life.

- ♥ **Developing a safety plan.** This is because domestic abuse affects not only current relationships but past ones too. So even if you have been able to leave that relationship, statistics say people affected by family and domestic violence may still live in fear for themselves and their family, even when they have left a violent relationship. PLEASE STAY SAFE.

♥ **Stay Active.** Were you forced to give up your hobbies or your job in your previous relationship? Now is the time to rediscover your old interests and to create new ones. Discover things that engage you and excite you, make them a part of your life and take pleasure in giving your life new direction and purpose.

♥ **Don't Be Ashamed.** It's crucial to the moving on process that you learn not to feel ashamed of your past relationship. Remind yourself every day that it was not your fault, you were not in control and that you did not deserve what happened to you. Repeat after me, "I am a good person. I did not deserve what happened to me but it's behind me now and I'm free to move on with my new, reinvented life."

♥ **Seek Counselling and/or Divorce and Abuse Recovery Coaching.** Even after taking these initial steps, it's common to find yourself feeling low and depressed after ending or escaping from a violent relationship. A counsellor can help you re-discover who you are as an individual by offering empathy and support to help you overcome feelings of low self-worth and shame. A divorce and abuse recovery coach can help you plan for a happier, independent future by making goals and creating steps to achieve your small and long-term objectives to help you devise life plans, reframe recovery goals and a come up with a future-driven vision. You can also seek professional help from your GP especially if you believe your mental health has been affected. Emotional abuse in particular is part of the power and control concept and is a form of brain-washing that can slowly erode your sense of self-worth, security and trust in yourself and others. In a lot of ways emotional abuse is worse than physical abuse because it slowly disintegrates one's sense of self and personal value. It can cut right to the core of your being, which can, without help after divorce, create lifelong psychological scars and emotional pain. If this is you, PLEASE SEEK HELP, you can and will recover and be reinvented.

♥ **Last but not least – Remember:**
  - You are Lovable.
  - Your freedom of choice has been restored – You can choose one thing today and another thing tomorrow.
  - You are powerful beyond measure.
  - You can now hold your own space to learn, grow and adapt at your own pace.
  - You do not have to accept or absorb lies, even if the lie has a grain of truth to it.
  - You are absolutely phenomenal.

Career Reinvention

There are so many reasons why you may want to choose a new career after your divorce. Here are just a few of the most common:

♥ Your husband didn't allow you work.

♥ You need a higher salary to take care of your home and children.

♥ You need the independence.

♥ You need a career that makes you happy.

♥ You need to take a step away from the people in your job (perhaps you worked with people who knew your husband or you worked with your husband).

♥ You didn't like your old job anyway.

Whatever the reason, now is the perfect time to take stock of what you want from a career and create a plan that will enable you to bounce back, become reinvented and ready to create a happier life. Some of you may not have looked for a new job for quite a while and might feel a little intimidated at the prospect of looking for new opportunities; some of you may still feel that a woman's place is not at work, but things have changed. This is the 21st Century and it's a woman's world.

More women are starting and successfully running small businesses than ever before; more women are leaders of big corporations and more women love their jobs, so you can too!

Advances in technology and the internet have opened up a whole range of new possibilities including flexible working and working from home, allowing you a greater choice over what you want to do and more flexibility when it comes to working around your children.

The first step to career reinvention is to make a list. Write down the following:

- ♥ **What skills do you have?** – Dig deep. A polite telephone manner and the ability to use a computer can be enough.

- ♥ **What hours can you work?** – Think about school drop offs and pick up's, spending time with friends and family and leaving some time for yourself.

- ♥ **Do you want to start a new business?** – Do you have an invention or a business idea that you're passionate about?

- ♥ **What's your dream job?** – The thing you've always dreamt of doing and are most passionate about.

Once you have your list you will have a clearer idea of whether your dream job is attainable based on the hours you are available to work and the current skills that you have. If you don't have the skills needed, learn them. You can take online or part-time courses to help you or look for volunteer work to get some experience.

Perhaps you can only work a few hours a day around your children's schedules. You may want to consider flexible working or childcare. In 2015, the government reviewed UK working regulations and increased the entitlement for flexible working. Everyone now has the right to request flexible working from their employer, especially parents.

Alternatively, have you thought about working from home? A lot of employers have made the transition to off-site workers to increase productivity and lower overhead costs like desk space and fixed phone lines.

You could also consider working for yourself as a freelancer such as a Virtual Assistant.

Virtual Assistants are growing in numbers. You only need a computer, internet connection and a telephone, along with a professional, friendly manner to get you started. You can choose what hours and which clients you work with and set your own hourly rates. There are even sites where you can source new customers such as People Per Hour, Upwork and Fiverr. If you'd like to start your own business, don't feel intimidated by paperwork. There's lots of support online to help get you off to a good start or you can find a local start-up support group that will help you work through the steps of getting your business off the ground.

If you crave the buzz from working in an office or shop, brush up on your interview skills and re-write your CV. Even if you haven't worked for a while, polish off your CV to include any extra skills you have, any volunteer work you've done and to clearly express why you want the job.

There are so many opportunities out there. You just need to look for them and don't give up at the first rejection. Take a deep breath, believe in yourself and be prepared to work hard.

Take the process in stride; it is all part of your Believe and Live Again recovery, bounce back, transition and reinvention journey from being a "we" to becoming a "me".

Perhaps you worked part time or volunteered while married. Maybe you took on a low paying role, even though you were highly qualified for a better job, so as to have quality time to manage the home and raise the children. Perhaps you never ever entered the job market but you worked full time at home because your spouse was the main breadwinner. Perhaps your spouse was the stay at home Dad because you had a high powered job and were bringing home the bacon

In my experience as a divorce reinvention and abuse recovery coach, the need for career reinvention or re-employment as it were of a "stay at home" mum is quite prevalent. This is usually because of the reduction of finances and family standard of living as a result of scaling down to a one person income family.

Interestingly enough, research has indicated that the potential lack of sufficient income post-divorce comes as a surprise for many divorcing couples, especially we women, as the focus is typically between you and your spouse.

Divorce can result in all kinds of inherent financial difficulty affecting equities in the family home and how this is divided, pensions, savings, other assets and even bills as well as debts too.

Understandably, if this is you, you may have many concerns and be very scared about re-entering the job market.

Please don't be discouraged and don't quit; don't be defeated before you have even started. Rise to the challenge, put your hands to the plough and rebuild and reinvent your life financially after divorce. I really believe that if you are able to rise to this challenge, even if you rebuild up a career that earns a fraction of what your spouse earned, you would have regained your power and self-respect and become happier and better adjusted post-divorce.

Here are some belief systems and strategies to help you on your career reinvention journey after divorce.

- ♥ Don't beat yourself up about being scared. This is your new reality so being scared is perfectly normal. I have reinvented my career several times over and at every stage I was scared, ok petrified, wondering if I had made the right decision and would I earn enough for the girls and me.

- ♥ Age discrimination (which starts about age 40) and gender discrimination and even race discrimination are facts of life. I won't sugar coat this and say it is easy to get a new job or even to build or re-build a career after being out of the job market for a length of time. You may be feeling very vulnerable and unsure of yourself as you go towards the unknown. Again these are normal feelings to have. Keep your eye on the prize; your sole mission with razor sharp focus is to push through those feelings and realise your career building or job seeking goals. The best way to get through those feelings is by taking action.

- ♥ Never under estimate or belittle your talent, no matter how many job rejections you may get before you secure a job. Remember that at the very least, you are as talented, capable and bright as your ex-husband. That's why he chose you, right? Granted, you may at times feel demoralised. Never the less, own the fact that you do have a lot to offer. Look for work that takes advantage of your strengths. Be persistent. Always think well of yourself. Banish negative thoughts and limiting beliefs.

♥ The 3 P's – patience, passion and persistence – are essential. Keep in mind that as you embark upon your job search you will also be competing with younger people entering the job market; some maybe entering for the first time. Don't let this fact deter you; it is an obstacle but you are more than able to overcome this. The important thing is for you to be relentless with bulldog tenacity; it is almost like a numbers game in that getting your foot in the door may take some time. Be patient, passionate and persistent and you will make it. It is also a good idea to have your personal cheerleading group of friends and family for moral support especially if you get a job rejection; let it be water over a ducks back as you take a deep breath and say to yourself, "Next please".

♥ Be flexible and keep an open mind. If you have been out of the job market for some time or perhaps never worked, you will be surprised to know that there are a variety of things you can do for work that you have probably never thought about or even knew existed. Examples include: on the street market research, election mobile canvassers, administrative roles and virtual assistant roles, the latter is quite new and has emerged as a result of the increase in solo entrepreneurs, coaches and online marketers who are always looking for support. The wonderful thing about becoming a Virtual Assistant in particular is that it can be done from home around your children especially if you have very good IT skills and there is huge potential to skill up so as to meet the demands of your varying clients. You may also want to consider freelance work via Upwork.com or People per Hour or Fiverr.com. Peruse these sites for ideas in line with your skills. You can also look for adverts in your local newspapers, shop windows, recruitment agencies or even your local job centre where a job advisor can give you more ideas on what could be a could fit for you.

♥ Talking about skilling up, you may want to consider going back to school to do a course relevant to your chosen career or perhaps embark upon some short-term training for a career. There are a plethora of short-term training programmes to gain entry into many careers, including in the medical and IT fields, many of which are available on the internet. The secret is be realistic, be focused and stoic, choose a job route that you think will be a good fit, that you will enjoy, and will lead to a fairly quick result.

♥ On the other hand you may be considered over qualified for the roles you are going for on account of age and profession and experience. I talked about age discrimination earlier. Don't let that deter you. Perhaps the story of Alice Solomon will inspire you:

A new Career after Divorce –
One Woman's Story: The Making of a "Gorgeous Grandma"[7]

At age 45, I had a terrible divorce. I use the word terrible because it was something I had neither expected nor wanted. After 25 years and two college-age sons, my husband phoned me from out of town to say he was not coming home. He hurt me so incredibly by walking away without even talking about it that I could not forgive him. I had been so tuned in to his needs that mine were secondary for 25 years.

What was I to do? What did I want to do?

While married, I had returned to college, which made him unhappy – even though I had given his approval. After the divorce, I finished school because I did not know what else to do.

I was graduated at age 50, cum laude, and was very proud of my achievement, but after spending years as a struggling student, I was lonely and at odds with myself. I sold our big, suburban home and moved into a one-bedroom apartment in Boston. I thought a new environment would refresh my life and help me start anew.

It didn't work.

Looking for the ideal situation, I held a few jobs over the years and moved from city to suburb again. Each time I interviewed for a new position, I felt overqualified, over-educated or discriminated against because of my age. Out of desperation, I decided to work at an upscale boutique department store. Although I did not like that either, I needed the money.

Ironically, from this job came many subsequent changes. To avoid boredom at work, I began to write newsletters to my customers who were mostly over 50 and unhappy with themselves. My inspiration to write a book came from dealing with these women on a daily basis. I decided one evening that I had a lot of information I wanted to share and that if I were going to do anything worthwhile in my life, I had better start now.

The following day, I purchased a computer and began a computer refresher course at my college. I then began an outline for a book, spending many nights researching and writing until 1 or 2 in the morning. When I told a newspaper friend about my project, she had her editor review a few articles and, lo and behold, almost overnight I became a newspaper columnist. Within a year's time, I was syndicated and my column, "A Guide for Gorgeous Grandmas," had a readership of over 150,000.

The real change in my life occurred when I returned to the career office at Wellesley College. Because of the encouragement of the Director at that office to do the book and any other projects related to "Gorgeous Grandmas", I began to smile again – perhaps the first real smile I felt in my heart for many years. I had found a calling, a purpose, a raison d'etre. And someone believed in me and my work! It was almost too wonderful to be real.

What brought these changes in my life? It was the recognition of my self-worth from my new identity as a writer plus the ongoing encouragement I received from the Director of the Career Office. I woke up, finally, to realise my value as a

person, not merely as a wife. I recognized that I had educated myself, experienced the highs and lows of being single and very lonely, and I had finally found a genre through which to express myself and feel valued.

I decided not only to finish my book but also to mount a website where women over fifty would be celebrated, respected and appreciated.

– Alice Solomon

Wow! Isn't that powerful – **Learning point:** IT IS NEVER TOO LATE!

♥ Perhaps you are entrepreneurial in nature; maybe you managed the books in the family business while you were still married and the desire to now set up your own business appeals to you. As a serial entrepreneur myself, my advice would be to do your due diligence in terms of product or service, target audience, route to market, initial investment required, income, and expenditure to stay afloat. Tread carefully.

♥ Talking about career reinvention, a year after my divorce – I started an online "After the storm, what next?" divorce support group comprising like-minded people just like me from around the world – with the shared experience of being people of faith and being divorced. We grew and became stronger in our shared bond, we reviewed recommended books, did research, used online tools, set new goals, and had joint accountability. And guess what? We healed and became each other's keepers. Through this wonderful experience, I was able to gain a lot of valuable insight into what works and what does not work for people after divorce. Although I didn't know it at the time, this was to become the genesis of – taa daa! Believe and Live Again.

Arguably, starting your own business has a lot of appeal and I get that, because you don't have to get a job, because you can create it for you and for others too. Setting up a new business is very appealing but from my own experience, it is not always roses. There are thorns at times too, yes! There are some down sides. The main one being cash flow. An ideal position would be having a significant divorce settlement you can fall back on while building the business or a reasonable amount of savings to invest into your new business while waiting for it to grow and begin generating an income on its own. Unless you have the right level of knowledge, entrepreneurial mindset and business experience or training, your new business may not generate the level of income you need or will fizzle out. If you don't have any start-up capital, it may be a good idea to secure a job first and then start your own business after you've built a career or saved some capital

♥ Whatever route you decide, whether going down the job market or setting up a business, you will become much happier and more fulfilled once you have achieved this goal. When a marriage ends, we all lose a great deal no matter who decided to end it. However, getting a job or starting a new business can hasten your emotional healing and can generate self-satisfaction. Achieving success in the outside world is a major accomplishment where you will be modelling independence and self-reliance to your children, both your daughters and your sons. Becoming independent and in control of your own life and career reinvention will actually make you feel very good about yourself. This inner strength will grow and enhance you going forward into new pursuits and into any new relationships you may embark upon in the future.

Healing, Restoration and Reinvention as a Woman of Faith

"Who shall separate us from the love of Christ?
Shall trouble or hardship or persecution or famine or nakedness or danger or sword?
As it is written: 'For your sake we face death all day long;
we are considered as sheep to be slaughtered.' "

No, in all these things we are more than conquerors through Him who loved us. For I am convinced that neither death nor life, neither angels nor demons, neither the present nor the future, nor any powers, neither height nor depth, nor anything else in all creation, will be able to separate us from the love of God that is in Christ Jesus our Lord. Absolutely nothing can separate us, including divorce.

My Christian faith has always been a big part of who I am; however, fundamentally this book and the services I offer through Believe and Live Again is open to all regardless of your faith, social status, orientation, or race. This is because in the final analysis, the pain, the trauma, the sense of abandonment, the stigma and the confusion after a divorce, separation or relationship breakup is gut wrenchingly real and the scars run deep, whatever your beliefs or core values may be. As a woman of faith I appreciate that we all need help and support at some point in our lives to get through the trials that come our way. I got my help through God and the people He used as his vessels. I know that same help is available for as many who may need it. God uses everyone, anyone and anything. Isn't that a comforting thought to know that that help is available when you need it most?

If you are a woman of faith and you are struggling to really comprehend the love of God in all this and also regain your positive sense of self and feminine power in Christ after divorce, rest assured that as He has done it for me, He will do it for you. Your healing, restoration and reinvention and everything else you need can be found in His Love that worketh within you.

Perhaps you are a woman of faith reading this and are wondering how you will ever survive after divorce. You find yourself often overwhelmed and ridden with guilt asking if God can ever forgive you. Can God ever love you again? So many questions and so many different answers. However, I want you to know that **Romans 8:35-39** is very clear and consistent when it talks about God's love for us.

"Who shall separate us from the love of Christ?
Shall trouble or hardship or persecution or famine or nakedness or danger or sword?
As it is written: 'For your sake we face death all day long;
we are considered as sheep to be slaughtered.'
No, in all these things we are more than conquerors through him who loved us.
For I am convinced that neither death nor life,
neither angels nor demons, neither the present nor the future,
nor any powers, neither height nor depth, nor anything else in all creation,
will be able to separate us from the love of God that is in Christ Jesus our Lord".

Absolutely nothing can separate us including divorce.

Woman of Faith, are you struggling to regain your positive sense of self and feminine power in Christ after divorce? Rest assured that all you need can be found in His Love that worketh within you. If you want to reacquaint yourself with the reality of God's Love, Jennifer Izekor's book *Seven Days with His Love Within* is, in my opinion, the most amazing and spiritually uplifting book for 2016 and will help in no small way to get you back in his presence.

Perhaps you often feel lonely. Loneliness is recognised the world over as one of the toughest problems for divorced people no matter their faith. As Jim Smoke and Edward Tauber advised in their book, you really need planned and intentional activities to help you when you are at your lowest ebb or when you are feeling lonely.

Some examples of coping mechanisms for loneliness are: calling friends, inviting people to come over, going out to public places, going to shopping malls, attending meetings or hobby groups – anything that gets you in touch with people. *"Remember, the loneliest place in the world is in an unhappy marriage where you are stuck. Being divorced, you now have options"!*

Exercise 11. **Loneliness Buster**

List some methods you have used and devise some new ones that you can use when you begin to feel isolated or down. This preparation will serve you well when you have those downer days.

- ♥ Be creative.
- ♥ What will you do?
- ♥ Where will you go?
- ♥ Who will you contact

I had been married for a little over 13 years when my ex filed for divorce. Like I said early on in the book, with hindsight, my marriage was fundamentally flawed from the get-go, but as a Born Again Christian, I devoured the Bible ferociously, I prayed, I cried, I fasted, had marriage counselling sessions with our pastor which interestingly, my "wasband" never attended, but I really believed that my marriage would work if I worked harder at it. Can you spot the anomaly there? *"If I worked harder at it."*

I was the first woman in my entire family to ever get divorced and what made it worse is that as a Born Again Christian, none of my close Christian friends had been through divorce either. I felt as if I stuck out like a sore thumb and was a failure.

I was brought up and had always believed that marriage was forever, that no matter what, stoically, you stayed together and eventually the storms would pass.

Divorce was just not for people like me, I thought. *"People like me?"*

My perceptions of divorce were quite frightful. It was that of parental alienation, domestic violence and serial infidelity, whispered gossip from work colleagues, church folk after service and school mums in the play grounds. I saw broken homes, traumatised children and at times the worst examples of human behaviour, not to mention eternal damnation in hell fire.

"No, divorce would never happen to someone like me": **respectable, professional, nice, friendly, loveable, accommodating, ever happy, Christian woman. *"No! Divorce could never happen to me….."***

Zina, Zina, Zina wake up, oh yeah! That's me…then I woke up and reality set in….and that my friends, is what they call History.

I became emotionally and spiritually devastated and didn't know where to turn. Woman of faith, if this is you? You will get through this, God still loves you, he never stopped and is able to heal and restore you to wholeness

When reality set in, I decided to devour and learn everything I could find about relationships and what it takes to heal after a divorce. It was then that I realised that a lot of what I was hearing from well-meaning friends, family, the church and even what I was telling myself – with its best intentions, I might add, was mostly wrong or in any event didn't really demonstrate the love and character of God.

If you are a woman of faith and you feel guilty, condemned or stigmatised by the church on account of your divorce; be encouraged: DIVORCE IS NOT THE UNPARDONABLE SIN.

You are probably all "Malachi'd " out – 2:16, having heard it over and over again *"God Hates Divorce"*. – God hates divorce because it hurts people. If you go back and read Malachi 2 again carefully, you will find that only once in the chapter did God say He hates divorce, but five times He refers to the treacherous dealings with one's spouse that leads to divorce.

It seems to me that many of us Christian folk in church spend so much time focusing on divorce and are quick to judge someone because they got divorced. We neglect to consider what may be the root cause of that divorce, what was going on before the divorce took place. We have no idea what could be going on behind closed doors in the privacy of their homes, the hell they were going through, the repeated deceitful and unfaithful treatment by their spouse and yet we judge. In all this, I want you to know that DIVORCE IS NOT THE UNPARDONABLE SIN. Lift your head up high.

Perhaps, you may be feeling doubly wounded. First by your ex-spouse who you trusted to be your covenant life partner, and then by the church that has shamed, shunned and treated you as a second class citizen. You feel as if your divorce is held over your head and is a stigma that you must carry for the rest of your life.

Interestingly, the church in general has been willing to forgive everything but somehow has treated divorce as the unpardonable sin and has condemned remarriage.

Again, if we go back to the Word of God, we can see that this stance does not appear to align with Scripture. If we take a look at Matthew 12"31-32, Jesus says, *"... every sin and blasphemy will be forgiven men, but the blasphemy against the Spirit will not be forgiven men."*

My fellow woman of faith, while we wait for the church to catch up, I stretch out my hand of fellowship, hope, restoration and love to you; do not let you or anyone else condemn you. Come to God's throne room of grace boldly to receive the same mercy, forgiveness and grace that Jesus demonstrated in the way He treated the woman caught in adultery and the woman at the well. Last but not least, "forgive you"

Reinvention, Dating and Remarriage

Are you struggling with limiting beliefs or stories about yourself that hold you back from trying new things? Do you have a hard time letting go and forgiving others?

Reinvention, venturing back into the dating scene and subsequent remarriage is never easy and often we encounter resistance. We don't want to let go of the baggage from the past that caused us pain.

But each time a major shift happens in our lives – relationship breakdown, leaving a job, moving, losing a loved one – we are given a choice to either take control of who we will become or risk never reaching our full potential.

Perhaps, you are asking yourself: "What can I do at this moment in time to help me discover the next phase of my life in terms of going back onto the dating scene?

> **"You're never too old to set another goal
> or dream a new dream."**
> **– C. S. Lewis**

If you are in the process of divorce or newly divorced, the last thing on your mind is likely to be remarriage. So why are we discussing it now? Statistics reveal that while 80% of divorced people remarry, almost 50% get another divorce.

I guess we (that is, you and I) don't want to make that mistake and go through this all over again.

Why do so many remarry and divorce again? Here is what research and statistics have shown regarding re-divorced people:

Many subsequent marriages fail because a previous divorce creates circumstances that lead us to remarry before we are ready. As a result, we marry the wrong person for the wrong reasons.

Divorced people often choose a new spouse from weakness rather than strength.

♥ You are still coping with all the problems of your divorce

♥ You marry out of neediness

♥ You repeat mistakes because you didn't learn from the previous marriage

♥ You marry too quickly – not allowing two years to heal or dating your prospective spouse for less than two years

♥ You ignore red flags you find in the new relationship

♥ You choose a person recently divorced, someone with many problems, or someone not ready to remarry

Would you want to marry someone who was in your present condition? I know I wouldn't. Then why offer that to someone else? Wouldn't you want someone who was happy and whole and had it together? Isn't that what you want to offer someone? Then you have to grow through your divorce and be ready to remarry.

Exercise 12. **Ready4Remarriage Test**

Go to www.believeandliveagain.com/ready4remarriage and download the test. Make a number of copies. Even though you may be far from being ready to remarry, take the test now. See how you perform. Work on areas where you score poorly. Take the test again in six months to gauge your progress. Avoid getting serious with someone until you score well on all aspects of the test.

Don't get married for the wrong reasons

As advised by Jim Smoke and Edward Tauber who are leading authorities in the area of Divorce Healing and Recovery having spent more than 30 years teaching divorce recovery to thousands of people in workshops around the world. In their survey of redivorced people, a shocking revelation was made. The survey uncovered that that many of the repeat marriages were doomed from the start! Why? Because many of the people surveyed, remarried for the wrong reasons. This resulted in choosing the wrong partner.

Exercise 13. **Considering a Remarriage Prospect**

If you have met someone who you feel is a good candidate for remarriage, question your motives, and ask yourself are you considering remarriage on faulty premises based on any of the following reasons:

♥ You have outstanding divorce problems that you have not been able to resolve and you believe that by marrying this person, you will be rescued.

♥ Perhaps, you want to make a point either to yourself or to your ex

♥ You are absolutely terrified of going back into the dating game and don't want to suffer from being burned out due to prolific dating. You feel lonely and getting remarried with cure this loneliness

♥ They say love is blind and in your case, the red flags are so bright and still, you choose to ignore them due to the euphoria of a new romance. You are bored in your singleness, you believe getting marriage to that special someone again will give your life meaning You fell under immense pressure from your friends, families, other relatives or a dating partner

♥ Because of your age and/ biological clock you feel it's time to take the plunge before it becomes too late. Perhaps you are considering remarrying because you feel either obligated, guilty of afraid.

♥ You believe you have found the one, your soul-mate at first site (online dating)

♥ For money reasons and you believe these problems will be solved by remarrying a rich or financially buoyant person

♥ For the sake of your children

♥ To be reintegrated into what you consider being a "couples' world"

Only contemplate remarriage when the following conditions exist:

♥ That you are actually in love with this person and not just in love with the idea of love.

♥ You are not desperate to remarry or need to be remarried but really want to

♥ You are going into a new marriage with the intention of giving more than you get

Using your journal write an honest statement about why you want to get married again. Do some self-evaluation to determine if any of the wrong reasons discussed above exist. Additionally, dig deep to ensure your contemplation to remarry is predicated on the conditions listed. I have provided some space below should you want to record your statement here too and/or instead of in your journal.

_____

_____

_____

_____

_____

_____

_____

_____

_____

_____

_____

_____

Only contemplate remarriage if you are sure you this is person for you. The mistakes below are the ones you need to avoid when choosing a new spouse:

1. Don't become romantically entwined with a person who has no intention, has made it abundantly clear and is not ready to get married again.

2. Don't become pushy and desperate with someone who has clearly shown signs of being hesitant about getting married again especially to you. Never try to be a good person or a saviour to another person through your quest to remarry.

3. Be very careful not to choose a person who has a lot of angst and unresolved issues that they want to burden you with through marriage. It will be very ill advised to marry someone with whom you share very little in common, especially in terms of visions for the future, values, dreams and histories.

4. Do not, I repeat! Do not go for someone who will put their children and/or pets before you or there is a strong indication that resentment, jealously and rivalry could exist between the children and you. Also, if you have children, the same is the case – put your new spouse first.

5. Avoid obvious "red flags" you are not a saviour, do choose a person with addictions or other serious problems. Do not choose a person you have to encourage or cajole to truly love you and does not show it.

Referring to your journal again, come up with a candid reasons and put it in the form of declaration statement why you want to marry this person. Ask yourself if there is a possibility you could be making any of the mistakes listed previously. Dig deep again to see if there are any obvious red flags you are ignoring. Write them down too!

Start your declaration:

I, **Name, aged‡‡‡** of sound mind and emotion, declare that I want to marry xxxx ppp because...
I also declare that the following red flags exists:
Or I also declare no red flags exist............ **(DELETE as relevant)**

_____

_____

_____

_____

_____

_____

_____

_____

_____

_____

_____

_____

_____

_____

How to Know When I am Ready to Date and Remarry[8]

This is a very frequent question that I get asked as a divorce recovery and reinvention coach. Here are some questions to help you find this out for yourself:

Q. Do you feel like you are ready to re-enter date field? *Y/N*

Q. What thoughts come to mind when you think about dating?

_____

_____

_____

Q. Are you scared to date again? *Y/N*

8 **Source and inspiration:** *Finding the Right One After Divorce*, Edward M. Tauber and Jim Smoke, Harvest House Publishers, 2007

If yes, what fears do you have about dating? Write them down.

_____

_____

_____

Q. Have you taken any active steps to meet someone or are you just waiting for the doorbell to ring or for someone to just approach you in the street?

_____

_____

_____

Q. Do you believe there is someone out there for you? *Y/N*
If not, why not?

_____

_____

_____

Q. Are there any false assumptions or excuses you are using that prevent you from dating? *(No one wants someone my age, I am not attractive, I have too much baggage, I am too busy to date, I can never trust anyone again, I'm too fat, too skinny blah, blah, blah.)*

_____

_____

_____

Q. Are you willing to commit right now that you will wait at least two years after the divorce before you get serious with someone so that you will enter a relationship from a position of strength rather than weakness? *Y/N*

Q. Finish this statement: "When I think of remarriage, I _____

_____

Forgiveness

"No longer will they call you Deserted, or name your land desolate.
But you will be called Hepzibah, and your land Beulah;
for the Lord will take delight in you."

Isaiah 62:4

What can I really add regarding forgiveness that we don't know already? If the truth be told, many of us believe in, especially when we want to be forgiven. The challenge I have found in my experience ad in my personal walk is that sometimes it seems just too abstract a concept to put into practise. What is even more interesting is the fact that even those who feel as if they **understand forgiveness and "do** forgiveness" although they may be reluctant to admit it, they also find it a challenge. It is like a weight that you just can't shift, so you decide either ignore or forget all about it, believing the pain, the hurt, the disappointment, the anguish, and the disillusionment will ebb away and you will be fine again...but guess what? It doesn't. And if we don't take drastic intentional steps to get rid of the root of unforgiveness in our hearts, we can remain stuck in the past all through our lives, even when we are able to mask

We all need a heart that is free and open as well as a mind and a clear conscience in order to embrace the new and to Believe and Live Again a life of love, purpose, clarity, and peace.

I can hear some of you say, *"Zina, it is easy for you to say, you don't understand what I went through, the pain, the hurt, the loss – I can forgive... maybe one day,,, but I WILL NEVER FORGET".* Or maybe you are saying, *"I CAN NEVER FORGIVE, full stop."*

"Forgiveness is not forgetting,
it is simply denying your pain the right to control your life."

– (Buchanan, 2009) Corallie Buchanan,
Watch Out! Godly Women on the Loose

Here are some Biblical scriptures I have found invaluable when it comes to the concept of Forgiveness.

1. *Matthew 6:12 NLT*

   "..and forgive us our sins, as we have forgiven those who sin against us..".

2. *Matthew 6:14-15 NIV*

   For if you forgive men when they sin against you, your heavenly Father will also forgive you. But if you do not forgive men their sins, your Father will not forgive your sins.

   Colossians 3:13 NIV

   Bear with each other and forgive one another if any of you has a grievance against someone. Forgive as the Lord forgave you.

   Ephesians 4:31-32 NIV

   Get rid of all bitterness, rage and anger, brawling and slander, along with every form of malice. Be kind and compassionate to one another, forgiving each other, just as in Christ God forgave you.

3. *Forgiveness is not a one time event, be prepared to forgive over and over again.*

   Matthew 18: 21-22 NIV

   Then Peter came to Jesus and asked, "Lord, how many times shall I forgive my brother when he sins against me? Up to seven times?" Jesus answered, "I tell you, not seven times, but seventy-seven times."

The learning point for all us here is that when we choose to forgive, it is more for ourselves than for others, especially in terms of our relationship with God and our spiritual growth in Him.

Chapter 21.

PHEW! REINVENTION FROM 'WE' TO 'ME'

"You're never too old to set another goal or dream a new dream."

— *C. S. Lewis*

January 17 2012

Dear Journie,

"The LORD our God spoke to us in Horeb, saying: "You have dwelt long enough at this mountain." Deuteronomy 1:6

Today at work was surreal. You know, I have been ok but today I was thinking about perfume. Yeah I know, I got Flowers by Kenzo as one of my Christmas presents from the girls. It brought back memories of how my wasband used to buy me perfume; he bought me Flowers by Kenzo at "duty free" on his way back from Germany in 2002. That singular memory set me off. It took me quite by surprise, I thought I was over my divorce. The next thing I realise I was sitting on the office toilet, with my face buried in my hands, and tears soaked in mascara rolling down, I was sobbing uncontrollably.

"God! Get me out of this wilderness, there has to be more to my life than being married, being divorced and then dying".

Suddenly, as if to answer to my cries, someone rushed into the next cubicle and sat down with a huge roar of relief. Journie, hearing those loud bodily noises, which I thought could only emanate from a wild animal and not a fellow woman like me, I stopped crying and it was at that exact time that I became aware of a silent stench beginning to waft itself rapidly in my direction.

Oh my days! Journie, I flushed the toilet and hastily hobbled out to the mirrors to fix my face; I say wobbled because I had sat on the toilet so long, that I had developed leg cramps and my feet had gone numb. I started laughing at myself uproariously and I dare say, the lady in the cubicle must have thought I was laughing at her. Personally, I felt as if this was a message from God that just like the people of Israel, I had dwelt on that mountain of pain and grief long enough and my life was developing cramps and becoming numb.

Journie, guess what? I feel a resolute resilience rising up within me, a strength, a conviction that I need to do something about it and this is the time to do it - now and fast, thank you Father God for always being there for me.

The title of this book is predicated upon Reinvent YOU. In fact the common thread throughout is the need or quest for reinvention and how to do it after divorce or a relationship breakdown; to find you, to uncover the mask of pain, shame, stigma, fear, and loneliness.

As women, many of us cannot leave our homes without "putting our faces on", that is, without applying makeup. This could be foundation, mascara, eye shadow, eye liner, blusher and of course a bit of "lippy". Some of us use heavy makeup, some are more subtle. The fact remains that makeup is to beautify our outward appearance and no matter how deftly we apply it, we cannot disguise or mask what may be going on inside – our emotions.

I appreciate reinvention. Major life changes like divorce are never easy because your instincts and the status quo of what once was is doing its best to work against you and the change. The transition is painful but when you learn to focus on your future self, you'll be surprised at what you can achieve. Believe and Live Again was born out of that "toilet Damascus" experience and the rest, as they say, is history.

I repeat: *"You're never too old to set another goal or dream a new dream."* – *C. S. Lewis*

To your own future be true

Before you can reinvent yourself, you have to know who you currently are. I know, from my own personal journey how important it is to re-establish your own self-identity, embrace your strengths and weaknesses, discover you passion and rewrite your own story of life. As women, to begin that reinvention journey after divorce or even after some other traumatic adversity, it is crucial that we know who we are currently, the need to have an understanding of our strengths, our weaknesses and what we are passionate about can never be over emphasised. My charge to you as you near the end of this book is to embrace your own story and be brutally honest as you evaluate yourself and the effort required to achieve the reinvention that you seek.

It is a good idea to discuss your dreams with people who you trust and who care about you and know you well. People you trust to be honest with you about your strengths and weaknesses. They can help you gauge your skills and pinpoint your true passions.

Before you can reinvent yourself, you have to know who you currently are. I know, from my own personal journey how important it is to re-establish your own self-identity, embrace your strengths and weaknesses, discover you passion and rewrite your own story of life. As women, to begin that reinvention journey after divorce or even after some other traumatic adversity, it is crucial that we know who we are currently, the need to have an understanding of our strengths, our weaknesses and what we are passionate about can never be over emphasised. My charge to you as you near the end of this book is to embrace your own story and be brutally honest as you evaluate yourself and the effort required to achieve the reinvention that you seek.

It is a good idea to discuss your dreams with people who you trust and who care about you and know you well. People you trust to be honest with you about your strengths and weaknesses. They can help you gauge your skills and pinpoint your true passions.

"If you don't go through a process of self-discovery, but just accept others' decisions, 10 years later you might find yourself saying, 'I don't think that's me,'" says John Mayer, a professor of psychology at the University of New Hampshire and the author of Personal Intelligence.

RELEASE, REFLECT, RENEW, REINVIGORATE AND REINVENT

From my personal experience, I can tell you that divorce recovery and reinvention requires laser focus and bulldog tenacity. Let's face it, it is a major, traumatic and very often unwanted shift that has occurred in our lives, a shift that means change. A change that means reinvention and guess what? Just like I did, you have to take your feminine power back, it is your responsibility now that you are re-singled to regain control of who you will become or risk never reaching your full potential.

I've had the opportunity to reinvent myself several times over in my life, a Practicing Lawyer, Project Management Consultant, Serial Entrepreneur, Career and Business Coach, Divorce Reinvention and Abuse Recovery Coach, Published Author and now on my way to obtaining my PHD in Coaching and Mentoring and becoming an ordained Minister.

A divorced single mother, a Victor(ia) after domestic abuse, I believe that I have no excuse and definitely no choice but to bounce back time and time again to impact my world and change lives for the better. I understand the principles behind the parable of the five talents and with mine, for as long as I live, I will utilise them to God's glory.

Now, this is not about your faith, although mine is my very foundation and the air that I breathe. It is about making sure that whatever negative wind may blow your way in your life time, that you refuse to be beaten, that you develop a deep rooted resilience, a buoyancy, and a sense of purpose so strong that your life counts for much more than your divorce, separation, break up, bereavement, sickness and all the other trials that come in between.

Like I said earlier, to Reinvent YOU has to be a deliberate act; It has to be intentional. You have to choose reinvention. To date, each time I have done it, even between the tears and anguish, I went into a new path deliberately and with foresight.

What I have learnt is that you cannot wait for your new future after divorce to find you; to do so would be to wait in vain, lost in confusion and sadness, or to get all scrambled up like an egg in a situation you definitely did not want.

As you read in my journal entry of 2012, one morning at work, sitting on the toilet, thinking about something as mundane as perfume, I had my epiphany moment. After struggling in and out for years with grief and loss, I arose from my robotic slumber and realised that I was having so much trouble moving forward partly because I had no idea what it was that I wanted to move toward.

I was thinking about my past and allowing it to keep me captive, but not actually thinking about reframing my future and aligning that with what I wanted for my new reality. Career-wise I had reached a plateau. I had achieved significant recent and relevant success in my IT Project Management role but still felt unfulfilled. The toilet scenario is what I call my 'kairos' moment, when I finally discovered and understood my purpose and my big 'Why.'

Kairos is an ancient Greek word meaning the right or opportune moment (the 'supreme moment'). Kairos signifies a period or season, a moment of indeterminate time in which an event of significance happens.

As a woman of faith, I have learnt that a 'kairos moment' is God's appointed time to act.

It is a moment in time when the Holy Spirit draws near to do a special work in and through a person or group.

Interestingly enough, that morning on January 17, 2012, I woke with a vision: a crowd of people from the life I needed to leave behind with the sun rising opposite them and me standing between the two, the sun beating down on my face.

I remember my vision – in 1994 – of me in a green dress on a stage addressing a large crowd of predominantly women – I hate green and having gone to a mixed secondary school, always felt more comfortable in the company of men. I think in my teens I was a bit of a tomboy or perhaps I wasn't too comfortable being a girl having grown up as the only girl among 3 brothers until I was 14.

Anyway, suffice to say that I didn't put too much meaning into it, but that vision did not leave me. Fast forward to today – I regularly address large groups of women... still hate green but absolutely love fuchsia pink. Lol.

In the vision, I decided, finally, to turn from the group and walk toward the sun, my new life.

That vision told me what I needed to hear—that I had to take control of my future instead of letting my pain choose for me.

In no particular order here are some steps from my Reinvent YOU journey that I believe you will find useful too as you move from a life of emotional pain into a life of emotional gain:

1. Have a clear about what you want in your new future.

It becomes very difficult to craft a new future without having a clear vision about what that would look like to you.

Whenever you can, take time out, sit quietly, close your eyes, and imagine the people, places, or situations that you need to leave behind. Now, imagine the new future that you want, whether it's simply a feeling, a group of people, or a situation such as a wonderful new job.

Imagine how it will feel to be in that new life. Have a picture of the hot sun coming up behind your future and the warm glow of the light which will be permanently radiant on your face.

Now, stand up, just for a moment, and silently acknowledge your gratitude for everything that came before; the pain, the divorce, the shame, the anguish, the sleepless nights, the fear, the fretting for your future. Thank your past, turn toward the sun, and with compassion and gratitude imagine yourself walking away from the past and into the future.

2. Write about your reinvention.

"And then God answered: "Write this. Write what you see. Write it out in big block letters so that it can be read on the run. This vision-message is a witness pointing to what's coming. It aches for the coming—it can hardly wait! And it doesn't lie. If it seems slow in coming, wait. It's on its way. It will come right on time".

Habakkuk 2:2, The Message Version

Imagine a scene from your reinvention. Let there be an intentionality about it, write about how you'd like it to play out. Where do you live? What do you get up to in the mornings, afternoon, and evenings? Who are your friends? What do you spend your days doing? Continue writing. Don't stop for as long as this exercise feels invigorating and exciting to you. You could write scenes, dialogues, lists, and plans; the list is endless and can be whatever you make it to be. The secret is to focus on what good looks like to you so as you write and envision, make your future come alive. Write about how it will feel to be there. Keep your writing somewhere where you will look at it occasionally. Feel free to add to it as you need.

3. Build Vision Boards

Vision boards are one of my favourite and most productive tools. I build one each year or sometimes just add to my current one. Vision boards are a wonderful way to surround yourself with visual reminders of the reinvented life you'd like to create. It could be a new car, a book launch, a business start-up, a product creation, a world cruise, a new job in a particular field.

The idea is to put objects or images of what you envision someplace where you'll see them every day. If it's a home, find a picture of a house that you love and put it near your front door. It can be anything that reminds you of what you're moving toward.

4. Project Manage Your Vision.

I love managing activities and tasks in my personal life like mini projects. I even have my daughters send in highlight reports of the progress they have made on a particular goal or activity that they have devised for themselves or that we have planned as a family. Sounds a bit uptight and over the top as I read it back, but really, I just believe it helps in having some structure and in ensuring you meet your goals, targets or deadlines for specific activities you care about.

On that backdrop, you might find it useful to put some structure around the building of your vision board, by perhaps starting with writing down what your vision is and writing it in the present tense using a narrative format. Do your best to be as specific as you can. This helps bring your vision to life in real time, giving a full picture of how your vision board will look once completed and so it becomes much easier when you actually come to building your vision board. In addition, managing the building of your vision board as a project will help you better understand the scope of your vision so that you are able to think things through exhaustively and be confident you have not left anything off.

> *Then the Lord answered me and said:*
> *"Write the vision and make it plain on tablets,*
> *That he may run who reads it.*
> *3 For the vision is yet for an appointed time;*
> *But at the end it will speak, and it will not lie.*
> *Though it tarries, wait for it;*
> *Because it will surely come, it will not tarry.*
> **Habakkuk 2:2-3 NKJV**

Chunk it up. You have written a vision of your future, now chunk it up or break it up into workable tasks and activities. Ask yourself "what do I need to do, every day, to create that vision?" Do you need to research world cruises and popular destinations or perhaps read reviews? Are you looking for a new job or perhaps you have never worked because you were the homemaker during your marriage? Do you need to meet new people? Search for a place to live in your chosen town?

Make it specific. Make a list of everything you need to do and a schedule for when you'll do it. Then do it and commit to keep doing it, one day at a time, until your project is delivered successfully.

5. Revisit that Vision of you Soaring High into your Future.

Each morning and before you go to bed at night, revisit that vision of you soaring higher and higher into your new future.

Close your eyes, inhale and envision the new you gliding into the rising sun, toward your hopes and magnificent dreams, reacquainting yourself boldly with your big "Why?" Stop for a moment to exhale, in readiness to receive all your new life has to offer and, as you do, ask yourself, "Why are these new possibilities and opportunities coming my way?"

I would be lying to you if I said reinventing YOU is going to be easy, because it is not. If that is not enough, more often than not, the process is rarely clear-cut, simple or even plain sailing. There may be occasions where you experience a lot of resistance often as a result of being unable to get out of our own way we somehow dig our heels in and refuse to let go, even when whoever caused us pain is long gone. If that is not enough, the faulty stories and limiting beliefs we have about ourselves keep resurfacing time and time again, attempting to hold us back from embracing the new that so desperately wants to come through.

Don't let anything stand in your way of embracing this newly reinvented life, no matter the resistance or struggles you may encounter on your journey.

Every time you find yourself slowly slipping into old habits such as crying yourself to sleep and becoming withdrawn so that you end up isolating yourself, or perhaps you find yourself coming up with creative excuses for not attending that party, wedding or even a networking event, looking for work, procrastinating on something that could your emotional wellbeing, advance your career, improve your health, your finances, my advice would be not to invest time wondering why or beating yourself up.

Instead, take a time out. Stop and ask yourself this question, "What can I do right now in this moment in time to ensure that I keep moving on and forward?" You may find it more effective to write your answer to this million pound question down. The important learning point here is to ensure you listen to yourself, that you practice mindfulness and become more self-aware and pay attention to your answer. Then, no matter what you feel in that moment be it pointless, hopeless, useless, defeated, deflated, lonely, confused, tired, self-critical or disappointed, do something, anything to keep up the momentum; be as creative about it as you need to be. As long as it is what works for you. Do it- even if it's just one small thing. Mark Twain said, "Courage is not the absence of fear; it is acting in spite of it."

During a bad marriage, many of us dream of a future that's very different from our present lives, I know I did. However, once divorced, too often, we give up on our dreams when in reality this is the time that we need to push harder and be persistent. It is at this time that we need to really assess our present and where we would like to see ourselves in our future so that we are able to devise realistic and effective strategies to make it happen. We need to relentlessly pursue and ensure we achieve the new goals we set for ourselves during and after divorce so we can end up with a future we really want and not the one we don't.

Choose to be boldly audacious, resilient, unapologetic and positive instead of letting your fear reinvent your future for you. Here's to the Reinvented YOU!

How to maintain your new "Me"

Hear me, you have the answers within you.

So I encourage you to have confidence in your knowledge and wisdom. Believe that you already possess many of the answers that you are seeking for the new Reinvented YOU. I know you are able to make sound decisions when you listen to your inner voice and the still small voice of God whispering in your ears.

I faced my past. I took responsibility for my actions and grew from my divorce to recognise the patterns that I wanted and needed to change for my new beginnings – the "Reinvented Me". So I say to you, face your past, take responsibility, grow from your divorce. Find gratification in your accomplishments and the challenges that you are able to overcome along the way. Review your successes as this will undoubtedly inspire you to keep learning, growing and glowing.

Accept your feelings. Treat yourself with compassion whenever you get angry or sad. In the same vain, look for the underlying causes so you can address them at a more opportune less emotive time. Examine your beliefs and revise assumptions that may be holding you back. I charge you to only choose to interpret situations in a way that helps you to move forward into the REINVENTED YOU!

Pay attention to your body because, as I have found, healthy habits will help you to stay fit and manage stress. If you do seem under the weather, take time out….visit your doctor or simply REST…don't be a super woman. Just do all you can to respect your needs, care about your physical, mental, emotional and spiritual well-being.

Evaluate new information and feedback. Be vulnerable, discuss ideas with others. Like I said earlier, it is good to talk. Keep up with news that can enhance your new life and always be grateful for outside assistance while determining what is suitable for you and what is not.

Practice mindfulness. Increasing your self-knowledge and awareness allows you to hear your inner voice so that you are able to screen out distractions and clarify your values.

Last but not least, connect with your faith. For me, I cannot over testify of God's never ending presence, amazing grace and faithfulness all through my life especially during my marriage, my divorce and my subsequent recovery and healing. If you don't know Him, you might want to check and find out for yourself. What I can say is that **the Bible was and continues to be my guide providing a sure foundation for my convictions – in Him I am always secure.**

Every moment is precious, time is precious. As the days go by, you will be nearer to putting the past behind you, and moving towards a happier life after divorce.

A happier life that will truly allow you to BELIEVE, HEAL AND LIVE AGAIN! Congratulations to reaching your "Me". Welcome to the REINVENTED YOU!

I hope that this book has given you some new ideas and insights on how best to cope with the particular difficulties or turmoil you might be going through. I hope that by sharing my personal experiences I've helped immeasurably with your wonderful journey of discovery to a better YOU with boundless opportunities and made you aware that you are, by no means, alone.

Most of all, I hope that this book has emphasised that, just because you might feel lost or emotionally drained right now, there is still an opportunity to learn and grow. Things can most certainly change so see this period as a temporary break and a chance to plant the seeds for your new horizons – a complete transformation in definition from Divorcee to a successful, confident elegant, vibrant and magnetic power house of a Lady worth more than rubies – a lady on a mission to take her world by storm.

Always remember to believe in yourself and there is no doubt that you can come out of your divorce as a stronger, more focussed and self-aware person, released, renewed, re-invented, reinvigorated and re-ignited with irresistible influence everywhere you go. Sister, just go ahead, choose to BELIEVE, HEAL and LIVE AGAIN.

Being divorced has not diluted my belief in "and they all lived happily ever after". I am a romantic at heart and have not given up on marriage or getting married again. With maturity laced with hindsight and wisdom, the words of Robert Anderson sum up my idea and belief in marriage:

> *"In every marriage more than a week old, there are grounds for divorce.*
> *The trick is to find and continue to find grounds for marriage."*
>
> *~ Robert Anderson*

"There is hope for your future," says the LORD. *"Your children will come again to their own land."* Jeremiah 31:17 NLT

EPILOGUE

He was incredibly charming, gregarious, popular, principled, a 6ft 4in. hunk of a man and wonderfully good looking. When we first met he was very attentive, helpful, friendly, and considerate and appeared very loving; an altogether wonderful person, he really seemed to understand me in a way that few others did. I was floored, hook, line and sinker – totally in love.

My 'wasband' appeared so perfect for me, the man of my dreams, that I became blind to everything else. He came across as a strong Christian, a traditionalist with firm beliefs. If he heard of anyone being unfaithful, he'd get very angry to the point of almost madness so much so that I would have described him as family oriented.

We met in 1995, introduced by a mutual friend while studying in the library, and like a whirlwind, in spite of the many red flags, we got married in 1996.

Reality set in and I soon discovered that my 'wasband' was often moody like a lady suffering with regular PMS. It was literally like living with Jekyll and Hyde. I would be lying if I didn't say that the red flags of domestic abuse began to flutter frantically, but for some reason I was blinded by love. I often made excuses for his behaviour, I even blamed myself. My 'wasband', on the other hand, displayed a seemingly total lack of guilt or remorse irrespective of the effect his actions were having on me.

If that was not enough, he would often suddenly fly into a rage when I asked him even the simplest of questions and I would think to myself that I needed to work harder at not upsetting him and being a better more pliable wife. I needed to pray more; I would ask myself what's wrong with me? How come every one else had a happy marriage, even some of the openly horrid women I knew? All I wanted was a happy home and to make him feel happy to be with me.

Now with hindsight, you'd think that I would have recognised these red flags, but I didn't. I kept praying, I kept fasting, I kept reading Christian books on marriage, I practically slept with my Bible, kept praying again, kept forgiving, and kept hoping that everything would end up ok if I tried hard enough.

However, try as I might, it wasn't enough; he would treat me badly, manipulate me and play those dastardly mind games and somehow, I would still end up apologising for yet another misdemeanour. Then we would make up briefly. Looking back, I realise it was only because he wanted a "booty call". Soon afterwards, we would continue where we left off with him ignoring me again and then disappearing for days, only to reappear and act like nothing happened.

I would be worried sick, almost half expecting that a policeman would come knocking at the front door at any second to deliver fatal bad news. Then he'd come home and I'd ask him where he had been. He'd reply he was "on call", then he would say unbelievably hurtful things to me for no apparent reason like "why are you asking me so many questions, what I do or where I have been is not your business". Now I was getting stronger and would push back hysterically. He would often say (that is when he chose not to ignore me completely) "you are always crying and overreacting" or "you are too emotional".

I soon discovered he was leading a double life, he had loads of affairs but I was in denial, I just refused to believe that my traditionalist, staunch Christian husband would ever contemplate adultery, even though the signs were very evident.

His mobile phone was permanently in his possession and always on vibrate, he'd go into the toilet to take calls, he'd go out and not tell me where he was going or with whom. The list is endless.

He would also berate me in public and say it was a joke; he had no remorse whatsoever, no understanding of why I was so devastated. He was boastful, even, with no sense of the impact his words would have on me.

I regularly felt confused and drained with the constant turmoil of trying too hard to please him and it not being reciprocated. I shudder now, but looking back, I don't think I even tried to please God as much as I tried to please him.

Even after my marriage eventually disintegrated, I would often blame myself, thinking "if only I could have been a better wife".... you know the shoulda-coulda-woulda gremlins that try to haunt you. I had always prided myself with being a happy go lucky, personable, strong woman, but if the truth be told my abusive marriage and eventual divorce completely knocked me out for six. I kept up appearances for the sake of the children, my church, my friends and family, but even that was beginning to show cracks. For all my drama school antics, I wasn't always very successful at it, especially where the children were concerned.

Although young at the time, they knew, they felt and they saw Mummy was sad... Oscar winner I definitely wasn't.

Looking back, I was so busy trying to be this hard altogether superwoman that I refused to allow myself to go through the grieving stages properly. I really owned the divorced woman stigma all by myself, regardless of what the Church and my interpretation of God's view of divorce was.

However, a lot of positives emerged out of this ordeal. Firstly, it caused me to devour every self-help book I could on divorce and domestic abuse recovery – Christian and non-Christian. I also started counselling friends that were going through similar experiences either with rocky marriages or in a divorce situation with my new found knowledge and learning.

Being a big old soft romantic at heart and in spite of my own experience, I remain a firm believer in the institution of marriage – I am proud to say that I helped and continue to help a lot of couples get back on track.

I became that non-judgemental, impartial shoulder to lean on during their divorce journey – the Mackenzie friend. I have always had a reputation for telling it as it is and being objective, and many a time, I became the impartial friend both parties would turn to, which sometimes was a bit tricky. The beauty of it was that by not focussing on my issues, without my knowing or intention, my healing process had begun. Working with other people on their marital matters was extremely therapeutic for me.

Another amazing outcome was that the self-blame and loathing stopped as I begun to realise that it wasn't my fault after all. I had enrolled in a psychology programme and although I am not medical or in a position to give a definitive diagnosis, but through years of study, research and my own personal experience of living with him as his wife, I am able to recognise the red flags – the signs – albeit retrospectively.

Why am I saying this? Because unlike so many women, I am alive, I am not just surviving but I am thriving, living a life I did not even dream was possible, and even better, I am making a positive, transformational and reverberating impact in lives across the globe. Who would have thought..? Well he didn't.

But in the final analysis, it has nothing to do with what went wrong, why or how, but how you recover. This was a choice I made and must take full responsibility for it.

Here are some home truths to consider, again taken from Edward Tauber and Jim Smokes' book *Divorce Healing and Moving on after Divorce*.

- ♥ If you try to avoid mourning your loss, you will never emotionally heal.

- ♥ If you don't mentally detach yourself from your ex, you are likely to continue to have him or her control you or your emotions, sometimes in subtle but debilitating ways.

- ♥ If you don't fully accept that you are now single, you will not truly appreciate all that your new status offers you and you will stay stuck.

- ♥ If you don't learn what happened in your marriage that led to divorce and your role in it, you may be doomed to repeat the mistakes with the next person you seriously date or marry.

- ♥ If you don't take complete responsibility for yourself, you will be vulnerable to "saviours" who want to rescue and therefore control you.

- ♥ If you don't take responsibility for your children and learn to become a successful single parent, you will miss the opportunity to be important in their lives.

- ♥ If you don't learn to live in the present with a new life, you will stay focused on your hurtful past and be bound to the old problems.

- ♥ If you don't plan your future and take responsibility for executing the plans, you will never achieve your potentialities.

- ♥ If you don't learn how to get closure in your marriage, you will stay part in the old life and part in the new and drag the old baggage along into any new relationship.

- ♥ If you don't learn what you need to achieve to be ready to date and consider remarriage, you are likely to marry the wrong person under the pressures that divorce creates and find yourself unhappy or divorcing again.

So here I am today, 6 years on – have done all the above or a version of them so that I have been able to start Believing and Living Again. I regained my feminine power and positive sense of self and what's more, I have reinvented myself several times over and continue to do so.

My greatest testimony is the fact that I shine and share the same REINVENT YOU! from "ME" to "WE" message of hope, healing, restoration and purpose with women all over the globe and guess what? If I had to go through my divorce experience and the marriage that led to it in order to be an empowered blessing to all I meet, I would gladly do this all over again and again.

The BALA **REINVENT YOU! From** *"We to Me"* **90 day Bounce Back Programme** is available to sign up. Register today using the unique discount code *(ReinventME08)* **http://believeandliveagain.com/ZARIYCP**

This offer is only available to readers of this book until 31st March 2017. This programme will help you get unstuck, so that you are able to move on from the past to achieve your ambitions and re-gain your self-esteem. You will learn how to re-prioritise your life and get organised, have control over your finances, physical body and love life, enabling you to re-invent yourself into a better version of YOU.

If you are reading this book right now and wondering if this programme is for you, I offer a 45-minute complimentary coaching discovery session.
Go to: **www.believeandliveagain.com/contact**
or call **+44 2089383672** (24 hrs).

For additional support and downloadable resources to help you as you transition from "we to me" and recover from the grief of divorce to regain your feminine power and self-worth, visit the website at: **www.believeandliveagain.com/ free-downloads** and follow the instructions.

If you would like to order copies of this book for your organisation, ministry, charity, support group or group of friends, and/or would like Zina to speak at your event, please go to: **www.believeandliveagain.com/zina-arinze-reinvent-you-book/order**

Keep smiling, keep strong
and keep believing as you soar into the
REINVENTED YOU!

GLOSSARY OF LEGAL DIVORCE TERMS

I am acutely aware that you may have just gone through a divorce here in the UK and still have outstanding matters that are yet to be resolved between you and your ex-spouse.

On the other hand, you may be have just commenced the legal divorce process, and you are getting really confused or perhaps overwhelmed with all the acronyms, the terms and the myriad of different forms.

This glossary of legal terms is for you. I hope you find it useful wherever you are in your divorce reinvention journey.

Courtesy of **http://www.divorce.co.uk/divorce-resources/legal-terms-explained**

Access

This is now called contact. Arrangements for contact form part of a "child arrangements order".

Acknowledgment of service

A standard form (sent by the court with the divorce petition/matrimonial order application) that the respondent (and any co-respondent) must sign and return to the court to confirm that they have received the petition/matrimonial order application and saying whether or not they agree to the divorce.

Adjournment

In a family law context, this generally means a hearing is postponed to a later date.

Adultery

Sexual intercourse that takes place during the marriage between a spouse and someone who is not their husband or wife. This is one of the five facts or bases for getting a divorce.

Alimony

See maintenance.

Appeal

The process of asking a higher court to change the decision of a lower one.

Applicant

The person applying to court for an order.

Ancillary relief

This is now called financial proceedings or financial remedy application.

Answer

This is the formal defence to a divorce petition/matrimonial order application, rebutting the evidence. This may be necessary if there are allegations that are unnecessarily offensive, or if those allegations might prejudice discussions about parenting or finances if unchallenged. It is very rare for divorces to be defended.

Arbitration

An alternative to a judge deciding the case; introduced in early 2012. The parties can choose an arbitrator to rule on all or just some of the issues in dispute. The arbitrator's decision (called an award) is then made into a binding court order.

Arbitration service

A provider of arbitration services. We have a team of expert arbitrators. You can find out more information about them here.

Arbitrator

An arbitrator is a third party who reviews the evidence in the case (or a discrete issue within the case) and provides a decision that is legally binding on both sides and enforceable in the courts.

Barrister

This is a lawyer who spends the majority of his or her time arguing cases in court. Barristers also use that advocacy experience to work with solicitors in advising on possible outcomes. Also referred to as counsel.

Cafcass

This is the Children and Family Court Advisory and Support Service. A Cafcass officer assists the court with matters relating to children and, in disputed cases of contact or residence for example, may be asked to prepare a report for the court on what orders or action would be in the children's best interests.

Child abduction

The wrongful removal or wrongful retention of a child from his or her place of normal, day-to-day residence in breach of one parent's rights of custody.

Child maintenance

An amount that the parent not living with their child pays to the other parent in order to support the child.

CEV

A cash equivalent value (CEV) is the value of the rights accrued within a pension scheme (previously called cash equivalent transfer value).

Charge on property

This is sometimes used as a means of security if one spouse is awaiting payment of a cash lump sum on a delayed sale of a home. It works like an additional mortgage, but without interest being paid, and is usually expressed as a percentage of the value of the property. It gives the holder of the charge security because they know that they will be paid out of the proceeds of the eventual sale.

Chattels

Legal term for personal effects, usually house contents or personal possessions.

Child arrangements order

This order regulates arrangements relating to with whom a child is to live, spend time or otherwise have contact. It also relates to when a child is to live, spend time or otherwise have a contact with any person. It replaces contact and residence orders and brings together arrangements for both in one order. If you already have a contact or residence order, from April 2014, you will be treated as having a child arrangements order.

Circuit judge

In the family law context, this is a senior judge who deals with the more complicated cases in the Family Court. Appeals from magistrate's or a district judge's decision are heard by a circuit judge.

Civil partnership

The Civil Partnership Act 2004 came into operation on 5 December 2005 and enables a same sex couple to register as civil partners. Being civil partners enables the couple to have equal treatment to a heterosexual married couple in a wide range of legal matters, including on the breakdown of the relationship.

Clean break

An order of the court barring any further financial claims between the divorcing couple. A clean break settlement cannot include spousal periodical payments/maintenance (it can include child maintenance though). A clean break is only effective if the financial agreement is confirmed within a court order. The court has a duty in all financial proceedings to consider whether a clean break is possible.

Cohabiting/cohabitation

An arrangement in which an unmarried couple lives together in a committed personal relationship.

Collaborative law

An approach to dealing with family law issues such as finances on divorce and children arrangements built on mutual problem solving where the couple and their lawyers pledge to work together to negotiate an agreement without going to court.

Committal to prison

Sending a person to prison for breaching a court order.

266

Common law husband and wife

This is a common misconception; there is no such thing as a common law marriage. The rights and responsibilities of a couple who live together but are not married differ greatly to those of a married couple.

Consent order

A court order made by a court giving effect to the settlement terms that have been agreed between a husband and wife.

Contact

This was previously known as access. It usually refers to the arrangement for a child to visit or stay with the parent with whom they no longer have their main home. This can be by an order of the court in a child arrangements order or by agreement between the parents. Indirect contact means the exchange of letters, telephone calls or presents. Contact arrangements within a child arrangements order can also be made in favour of others, such as grandparents.

Contact orders

As from April 2014, contact orders no longer exist. They have been replaced with "child arrangements orders" which deal with contact and residence. When a child arrangements order deals with contact, it often orders the person with whom a child mainly lives to allow the child to visit or stay with the person named in the order. See also contact.

Co-respondent

A person with whom the respondent is alleged to have committed adultery. A person should not be named in a matrimonial application unless the applicant believes that the respondent is likely to object to the making of an order.

Counsel

Another name for a barrister.

Counselling

Specialist counsellors, with the right background, are able to help adults or children who are going through a separation. Other help can be provided by psychologists, therapists and family mediators with specialised training in working with adults or children within the family context. These professionals can be referred to as family consultants.

Family consultants can be brought into the collaborative law process to help spouses work out and articulate what they want, and to help and advise on ways to improve communication. Further support can help reduce conflict, help develop coping strategies for dealing with the emotional issues that may affect the family now and in the future and help everyone to move on with their lives following the divorce. Family consultants may also work with children, seeing them separately in appropriate cases, helping them to voice their thoughts, feelings, needs and concerns.

Court

The courts handle all types of family law disputes. From April 2014, there are only two types of court that deal with family law disputes. The Family Court will hear most cases and, depending upon the complexity of the case, the judge might be a magistrate (also called a lay justice), district judge, circuit judge or a High Court judge. Mostly, you will find your local Family Court based at your local County Court. A very few specific types of family disputes will be heard in the High Court.

Court fees

These are the fixed administrative costs paid to the court when making an application. Fees vary depending upon the type of application. If you are in receipt of public funding (legal aid), then the court fees are generally exempt.

Cost order

The court can order one spouse to pay the legal costs of the other. During a divorce, it is quite common for the respondent to contribute towards the applicant's costs. In most financial proceedings, there is a general presumption that each person will pay their own legal fees although costs orders can be made where there is "litigation misconduct", for example a person is dishonest about his or her financial position or ignores court orders.

Child Maintenance Service (CMS)

Replaced the Child Support Agency in November 2013. Its role is to make sure that parents living apart from their children contribute financially to their upkeep by paying child maintenance. It is intended to be used by only those parents who cannot come to an agreement themselves over child maintenance. All new applications for child maintenance made after November 2013 are dealt with by the CMS. There is a child support calculator on the Child Maintenance Options website.

Child Support Agency (CSA)

Replaced by the Child Maintenance Service in November 2013. It continues to administer all applications made before November 2013.

Custody

This is now called residence and forms part of the child arrangements order.

Decree absolute

The final order of the court, which terminates the marriage.

Decree nisi

The interim decree or order of divorce indicating that the court is satisfied that the marriage has broken down irretrievably. Six weeks and one day after decree nisi has been made, the applicant/petitioner can apply to the court to make decree nisi absolute (decree absolute) and the marriage is then terminated.

Directions order

A court order directing how the case will proceed (e.g. what evidence needs to be filed and what the timetable to trial is going to be).

Disclosure

This is the process of providing complete financial details about a person's capital, income, assets and liabilities. This is either done voluntarily or the court can order it. It is a necessary first step in any discussions about finance, even in mediation or in collaborative law. This is usually done by filling in a Form E.

District judge

A judge who sits in the Family Court. Most family disputes that end up in court are dealt with by a district judge.

Divorce

This is now called matrimonial order proceedings. This is the process which leads to the termination of a marriage. There are two orders: decree nisi and decree absolute.

Domestic violence/abuse

This has many forms including threats of and actual physical aggression, sexual abuse, emotional abuse, controlling or domineering behaviour, intimidation, stalking or passive/covert abuse such as neglect.

Divorce.co.uk

The most comprehensive free resource on the web, provided by the family lawyers at top 50 UK law firm Mills & Reeve. The information provided on the site aims to help families manage their way through relationship breakdown. Find out more at www.divorce.co.uk.

Duxbury calculation

Duxbury calculations are made to assist the decision as to whether or not a clean break is possible. The calculation produces a figure of what level of lump sum payment the recipient needs in order to spend the rest of their life at a certain amount of expenditure each year.

Equity

Refers to the net value of a property after mortgages or other charges are paid off.

Ex parte

This is now called without notice. It most commonly refers to emergency hearings that are conducted with only the applicant present at court. If the court makes an order at the without notice hearing, the judge will ensure that another hearing can be held quickly afterwards in order to hear the respondent's case and then make a final order. Often without notice hearings are used to deal with injunctions.

Family proceedings court

The name given to the division of the magistrates' court that dealt with family law matters. It was abolished on 22 April 2014.

FDA

First directions appointment: this is the first court appointment in financial cases and tends to be mainly administrative (family lawyers sometimes refer to it as a "housekeeping" hearing). The judge will consider what information is needed from both sides in order to progress the case. If the couple is able to agree the directions prior to the FDA then it may be possible to treat it as a financial dispute resolution (FDR).

FDR

Financial dispute resolution appointment/hearing: the second court appointment under the standard procedure in financial proceedings. This is an opportunity for the parties to negotiate on a without prejudice basis and with the assistance and guidance of a judge. Importantly, the judge who deals with the FDR cannot take any further part in the case if it does not settle at that hearing, other than to give directions for progressing the case to a final hearing. The FDR can, in more simple cases, sometimes be combined with the first appointment (FDA) to save costs and speed up progress.

FHDRA

A first hearing dispute resolution appointment: the first court appointment in a private law children application.

Final hearing

The trial and the final court appearance in all proceedings. A judge will hear the parties and any experts give evidence and will make a binding court order as a result. In limited situations there are grounds for appeal.

Financial proceedings

See financial remedy application. These are generally the court proceedings following a divorce to reallocate the income and capital of a family.

Financial remedy application

This used to be called ancillary relief. This is the application to the court for financial orders following a divorce. The court can make a variety of orders about the finances of a divorcing couple. These are lump sum orders, property adjustment orders, property transfer orders, variation of trusts orders, periodical payments/maintenance and pension sharing orders.

Five-year separation

One of the five "facts" or bases for getting a divorce, ie, the couple has lived apart for five years (no consent needed).

Form A

The application form sent to the court that begins the process of dealing with the financial claims on a divorce. It puts in place a court led timetable for financial disclosure and also sets a court date, which will either be an FDA or an FDR depending upon how much can be done beforehand.

Form E

This is the court form setting out a person's financial circumstances (called financial disclosure) as well as details about what orders are sought. It is about the same size – and as much fun – as a tax return. It is obligatory to complete and confirm the truth of this form in court led proceedings. It is often also used as a checklist for voluntary financial disclosure and in those cases where the parties are able to come to a financial agreement without needing the help of the court, directly or through mediation or collaborative law.

Form G

This is a simple form sent to the court before the FDA confirming whether or not it is possible to combine the FDA and the FDR hearing.

Forms H and H1

These are forms filed before each court hearing, which provide details of each party's costs and what has been paid towards them.

Former matrimonial home

The house in which the divorcing couple were living together before they separated. If it is owner occupied, it is often one of the biggest assets that has to be dealt with on divorce.

Get

A document made in a Beth Din (a court of Jewish law) dissolving a Jewish marriage following proceedings under Jewish law. It is handed over by a husband to a wife.

Injunction

An order of the court preventing or requiring action, usually made in an emergency.

Interim maintenance

See maintenance pending suit.

Joint tenancy

A form of joint ownership of land in which both parties share the whole title to the property. If one party dies, the survivor will own the entire property (the "right of survivorship").

Judicial separation

A formal separation sanctioned by the court, which enables the court to make orders about money and property but does not actually terminate the marriage.

Leave to remove

An application to the court for permission to remove a child permanently from England and Wales. This is now called permission to remove.

Legal Aid Agency (LAA)

Provides both civil and criminal legal aid and advice to those people who qualify for it. Due to government cuts in the legal aid budget, there are very few family cases which benefit from legal aid. However, you may be able to get legal aid if you have been the victim of domestic violence or if you are using mediation to resolve your dispute.

Legal Services Commission (LSC)

Now called the Legal Aid Agency

Litigant in person

A person acting on their own behalf without assistance from a solicitor.

Lump sum order

A fixed sum of money paid by one person to another. It may be payable in one go or in instalments. This is one of the financial orders open to the court to make when deciding a financial settlement on divorce.

McKenzie friend

An individual who assists a litigant in person in the courtroom.

Maintenance

A regular payment of money by one spouse to another under a court order or following an agreement. Spousal maintenance refers to maintenance paid from one spouse to another. It is possible to capitalise spousal maintenance by the payment of a lump sum to achieve a clean break. Maintenance can be secured on the assets of the paying party if there is a risk that the order may be breached. Those assets can then be sold to ensure the recipient's claim is satisfied. Those orders are rare. See also child maintenance.

Maintenance pending suit

In financial proceedings, a person can apply for interim periodical payments/maintenance, which is payable on a temporary basis while the proceedings are ongoing and before they are concluded. It is sometimes called interim maintenance or MPS. This is particularly useful if the financial proceedings are going to take some time to conclude.

Matrimonial order application

This used to be called a divorce petition. This is the document that starts the divorce proceedings. It sets out the basis for the divorce, i.e., whether it is based on unreasonable behaviour or adultery or a period of living apart.

MPS

See maintenance pending suit.

Mediation

The process through which independent mediators try to help a couple reach agreement about the arrangements to be made for children and/or finances following their decision to divorce or separate. It is sometimes wrongly thought to be a discussion about the relationship and whether a reconciliation is possible.

Mediation information assessment meeting (MIAM)

Before court proceedings can be issued – either about children or about finance – you will usually be required to attend a meeting about mediation to ensure you have information about the process. This is called a mediation information and assessment meeting (MIAM). This meeting can be a useful way of finding out more about mediation, although it is better to have explored the option of mediation before you decide that you want to start court proceedings.

Mediation service/s

A provider of mediation services. We have a team of expert mediators and you can find out more about them here.

Mediator

A third party who assists the parties to reach a negotiated settlement.

MIAM

See mediation information assessment meeting.

Mid-nup

A mid-nuptial agreement: an agreement made during the marriage. See post-nup.

Mirror order

A court order obtained in a foreign court, which reflects exactly the terms of an English court order. Mirror orders are generally obtained to enforce the terms of an English order outside England and Wales.

Mortgagee

This is usually a bank or building society, but it can be anyone who lends you money to buy a property on the security of the property.

Mortgagor

This is the borrower who obtains a mortgage.

Non-molestation order

An order prohibiting a person from molesting another person. The order usually prohibits one person from using or threatening violence or intimidating, harassing or pestering another person. The order can include the protection of children. Once a respondent is aware of a non-molestation order, breaching it is a criminal offence that is punishable by either a fine or a term of imprisonment. This often goes hand-in-hand with an occupation order or orders relating to the children.

Occupation order

An order regulating the occupation of the family home. A person can be excluded from the family home or from a certain part of it for a set period of time. If the respondent breaches an occupation order, if a power of arrest has been attached to the order, the police can arrest the respondent and bring them back to court.

Offer to settle

Offers to settle may be "open". This means they can be referred to, openly, in court and especially at any final hearing. Offers to settle may also be without prejudice, which means it is not possible to refer to them openly in court except at the FDR and especially not in any final hearing.

Order

A direction by the court that is legally binding and enforceable.

Parental responsibility

If the parents are married, or if the child was born after 1 December 2003 and the father is named on the birth certificate, both parents of a child have joint parental responsibility for that child before, during and after divorce or separation. This term describes all of the rights, duties and responsibilities which, by law, a parent of a child has in relation to that child. Aspects of parental responsibility include decisions about a child's religion, education, name and medical treatment.

Particulars

If a matrimonial order application for divorce is based on unreasonable behaviour or adultery, it has to set out details. This can be upsetting and, in some cases, offensive. It is best to try and agree the particulars before the matrimonial order application is sent to the court.

Pension

Cash and/or an income paid by the Government or a private company or arrangement on a person's retirement. Pension funds can be extremely valuable and may be an important part of any financial settlement, especially after longer marriages. There are three ways of resolving issues around pensions and provision on retirement.

Pension earmarking is arranging that, when a pension comes to be paid, a proportion of it is paid to the other party.

Pension offsetting is offsetting the value of the pension against some other asset such as the marital home.

Pension sharing is the splitting of the pension at the time of divorce, giving both parties their own pension fund.

Periodical payments

The technical phrase for maintenance or alimony.

Permission to remove

An application to the court for permission to remove a child permanently from England and Wales. This used to be called leave to remove.

Petition

See matrimonial order application.

Petitioner

Now called an applicant. This is the person applying for the divorce in the petition/ matrimonial order application.

Post-nup

The aim of a pre-marital agreement is usually to protect the wealth of one or both spouses and, if prepared properly, should be binding. If you are considering a pre-nup you should seek specialist advice immediately. You can also take steps to protect your position after the wedding, which may involve a post-nup/mid-nup. These are the same as a pre-nup, but made at any time after the marriage ceremony.

Power of arrest

This allows the police to arrest a person who ignores or breaks an order of the court. If your partner breaks the order and you call the police, they will ask to see a copy of the order to see if it has a power of arrest. Once the police have arrested that person they must bring them back to court within 24 hours. A power of arrest can only be attached to an occupation order and not a non-molestation order because a breach of a non-molestation order is automatically considered to be a criminal offence.

Prayer

The section of the petition that asks the court to make orders in favour of the petitioner.

Pre-nup

A pre-nuptial agreement (also known as a pre-marital agreement or contract) is made in contemplation of marriage, most commonly setting out the terms which are to apply between the spouses in the event of separation or divorce. Sometimes they can deal with arrangements during the marriage, upon separation/divorce and upon death.

Parent with care

A term that used to be used by the Child Support Agency for the parent with whom the child had his or her main home. The Child Maintenance Service now refer to the parent with care as the "receiving parent" (i.e. they receive the maintenance on behalf of the child).

Privilege

The right of a person to refuse to disclose a document or to refuse to answer questions on the ground of some special interest recognised by law.

Process server

This is someone employed to serve court papers. To prove that the papers have been served, the process server will normally swear an affidavit, which will be sent to the court.

Prohibited steps order

An order used to prohibit something being done to a child, for example, changing a child's surname or taking the child out of England and Wales.

Property adjustment order/property transfer order

The court's power to change the ownership of an asset. Usually, but not always, this will be in relation to property.

Questionnaire

A list of questions asking for further details about a person's financial circumstances. This is usually made in response to any gaps or omissions in someone's Form E in financial proceedings.

Relevant child

A child of the marriage, either aged under 16 at the time of decree nisi or aged between 16 and 18 and in full time education or training. A disabled and dependent child of any age will always be considered a relevant child.

Residence

This describes where and with whom a child lives on a day to day basis, or has their primary home. Previously termed custody although the legal consequences are different.

Residence order

As from April 2014, residence orders no longer exist. They have been replaced with "child arrangements orders" which deal with contact and residence.

Request for directions for trial

A specific application to the court which asks for the decree nisi to be made.

Respondent

The person who receives the divorce petition/matrimonial order application or some other application to court, such as in financial proceedings.

Sale of property order

Where a court makes an order for secured periodical payments (see maintenance),lump sum or property adjustment, it may make a further order for the sale of property to satisfy the earlier order.

Seal

A mark or stamp that the court puts on documents to indicate that they have been issued by the court.

Separation agreement

A contractual document that deals with the arrangements between a couple after their separation. Sometimes this is used when a divorcing couple are waiting for the two years' separation to elapse.

Service

The process by which court documents are formally sent to, and received by, the party to whom they are addressed.

Set aside

Cancelling a judgment or order.

Solicitor

A lawyer who advises a client and prepares a case for court. Specialist family law solicitors may also be trained as mediators, collaborative lawyers or arbitrators.

Special procedure

When divorce/matrimonial proceedings are undefended, the decree nisi and decree absolute can be issued without either spouse having to appear at court. Although called "special", in fact this is the normal procedure for most divorces. This is sometimes called a "quickie divorce" by the tabloids.

Specific issue order

An order determining a specific issue relating to a child, for example, which school a child is to attend.

Section 8 order

An order under section 8 of the Children Act 1989: namely a child arrangements order, a prohibited steps order and a specific issue order.

Section 25 factors

The checklist of criteria upon which financial remedy applications are decided.

Statement in support of divorce

This statement poses a number of questions aimed at ensuring that the contents of your petition remain true and correct and that there have been no changes in circumstances that may affect your ability to rely on the fact of (adultery/ unreasonable behaviour/ desertion/ two years' separation with consent or five years' separation) to support the irretrievable breakdown of your marriage. This statement has to be filed at court when you apply for Decree Nisi.

Statement in support of petition

A formal statement sworn on oath to be true by the person making it, usually in support of an application to the court. See also swear.

Statement of arrangements

The document that used to be sent to the court with the petition/matrimonial order application if the divorcing couple had children. As of 22 April 2014, it is no longer necessary to submit this document with your petition.

Statement of truth

A statement or other document containing facts verified as being true by the person making the statement. If the document is false, proceedings for contempt of court may be brought against the person who made the false statement.

Stay

To place a stop or a halt on court proceedings.

Strike out

The court ordering that written material or evidence may no longer be relied upon.

Swear

To declare on oath that what is being said or what is contained in a document is true. This is usually administered by a solicitor, notary public or a member of court staff. It sometimes incurs a small fee.

Talaq

Dissolves an Islamic marriage under Islamic law. It is a unilateral process whereby a husband rejects his wife by saying words to the effect "I divorce you".

Term order

Maintenance/periodical payments for a specified period of time. The term (or length) of the order can either be capable of being extended to cater for something unexpected happening or, alternatively, the court can order that the term cannot be extended.

Tenancy-in-common

This is one way of owning property jointly. The separate shares are agreed (usually when the property is purchased). If one of the owners dies, their share will form part of their estate and will not automatically belong to the survivor, unlike joint tenancy.

Two-year separation

The divorcing couple has lived apart for two years and the other spouse consents to divorce. This is one of the five facts on which a divorce can be based.

Undertaking

An undertaking is a promise given to the court or to the other party. Once an undertaking has been given to the court, it has the same effect as a court order. This means that, if it is broken, it will be seen as contempt of court and (in extreme cases) an application can be made for the person who has broken the undertaking to be committed to prison.

Unreasonable behaviour

This is one of the five facts on which a divorce can be based. Particulars of the behaviour have to be set out in the petition/matrimonial order application.

Without prejudice

Correspondence or documents that are marked "without prejudice" cannot be shown to the court. The purpose of allowing this is to encourage discussions about settlement. The only time a court can see without prejudice proposals is in the FDR hearing because this is a without prejudice hearing.

BIBLIOGRAPHY

1. Buchanan, C. (2009). *Watch Out! Godly Women on the Loose.* Mona Vale, Australia: Ark House Press.

2. Chapman, Gary, Campbell, Ross M.D. (2012). *The Five Love Languages of Children.* Chicago, USA: Moody Press.

3. Kubler-Ross, E. (1969). *On Death and Dying.* New York: Macmillianr.

4. Mayer, J. (March 2014). *Personal Intelligence.* New York, USA: Farrar, Straus & Giroux Inc.

5. Smoke, E. M. (2007). *Finding the Right One After Divorce.* Eugene, Oregon: Harvest House Publishers.

6. UK, T. L. (2016, December 16).
   http://www.lawsociety.org.uk/for-the-public/common-legal-issues/getting-a-divorce/

7. Retrieved December Friday, 2016.
   http://www.lawsociety.org.uk/for-the-public/common-legal-issues/getting-a-divorce/

Zina Arinze, fondly known as the Divorce Reinvention Queen, is a bubbly woman of faith, Radio Broadcaster and Talk Show host, a successful serial entrepreneur and the founder of Believe and Live Again where she provides Post-Divorce Lifestyle Coaching, Abuse Recovery and Reinvention Mentoring services for female professionals, women of faith, business women and female entrepreneurs from around the globe.

An active member of the Institute of Enterprise and Entrepreneurs, Zina sits on several boards and panels providing expert comment and advice to Business Schools, and Business Mentorship to SMEs and Charities.

Zina is also a Gender Equality and Woman Empowerment strategist having firm ties with UN Women Training Centre.

Zina wears many hats, a lawyer by training, specialising in family law and armed with an MBA, she is also an accomplished certified Divorce Recovery Coach, a prolific writer, corporate life skills trainer, A Youth and Business Mentor, and a successful IT Project Management Consultant with over 20 years experience in delivering multi million pound projects and capacity building gained from the Public, Not for Profit and Private sectors. Zina is also a well sought after motivational empowerment speaker and an exceptional devoted single mother to two amazing gifts, her teenaged daughters, Princess number 1 and Princess number 2.... phew!

But in all this, Zina's greatest call to fame is her Christian faith and being the world's No 1 Mum. She will always tell you – "I am a mum first, an incubator for our better tomorrows".

A firm believer in maximising every moment, she lives by the her mantra *"You are never too old to set another goal or to dream a new dream" – CS Lewis.*